Taiwanese Style
Chinese Cuisine

主　　　廚	黃德興、楊文典
烹 飪 協 助	財團法人味全文化教育基金會附設家政班
編　　　著	林麗華
翻　　　譯	Linda Hanna Chen
出 版 者	純青出版社有限公司　　　　郵政劃撥：12106299
	104台北市松江路125號3樓　　電話：(02)2508-4331
	網址：www.weichuan.org.tw　E-mail:we122179@ms13.hinet.net
版 權 所 有	局版台業字第3884號
	中華民國80年1月初版發行
	中華民國92年4月八刷發行
印　　　刷	中華彩色印刷股份有限公司
定　　　價	新台幣參佰元整

Author　　　　　Lee Hwa Lin

Translator　　　Linda Hanna Chen

Publisher　　　Chin Chin Publishing Co., Ltd.

3th fl., 125, Sung Chiang Rd.,Taipei, Taiwan, 104 R.O.C.

Tel:(02)2508-4331・Fax:(02)2507-4902

Distributor　　Wei-Chuan Publishing

1455 Monterey Pass Rd., #110

Monterey Park, CA91754, U.S.A.

Tel :(323)2613880・2613878　Fax:(323)2613299

Printer　　　　China Color Printing Co.,Inc.

Printed in Taiwan, R.O.C.

Copyright Holder　Copyright ©1990

By Wei-Chuan Cultural-Educational Foundation

First Printing, Jan., 1991

Eighth Printing, Apr., 2003

ISBN 0-941676-25-0

序

　　我國以烹飪術馳譽世界，近數十年，中國菜更風行全球。

　　中國雖地大物博，但因人口眾多，所以仍不免時有食物不足之虞。為了應付食物的匱乏，中國人數千年來以其累積的經驗，發展出一套物盡其用的方法。中國人認識其環境，自其環境取得食物，種類遠比他民族為多，且能充分予以利用。例如動物的食用，除食其肉外，兼及內臟等，為中國菜的特色。中國菜由於材料豐富，因此菜式也特別多樣，中國餐館所能提供的菜單，其種類通常都在外國餐館的二、三倍以上，這也許是中國菜特別受到歡迎的原因之一。

　　中國菜因地域不同，各具特色。較有名的有北京菜、山東菜、山西菜、四川菜、湖南菜、揚州菜、江浙菜、廣州菜、潮州菜……等等。台灣菜屬閩菜系統，所謂閩菜指福州菜和閩南菜，只是台灣曾有半世紀遭受日本統治，光復後又有大量各省人士遷徙入台，在社會文化各方面都受到相當的衝擊，因此現在的台灣菜，雖仍以閩菜為其主幹，實已摻有各地烹飪手法，成為一新的烹飪系統。

　　台灣菜的主要特色是調味清淡，刀工細膩，善使用酸甜作料，以湯菜取勝。台灣因屬海島，魚產豐富，故菜式以海鮮為主。烹調方法除傳統之蒸、炊、燉、煎、炒、炸、烤等外，更有承襲自日本料理之生吃或冷食。此外，台灣菜的另一特色是進補食療，佐以中藥材燉蒸，以利祛熱降火、滋補強身，則為我國傳統食療法的延續。

　　味全文化教育基金會以台灣菜既為我國烹飪藝術之一新烹飪系統，特別紀錄台灣菜食譜：海鮮類二十六，肉類十七，蔬菜類六，蛋、豆腐類七，湯類九，點心類八，另，粥品五，合計七十八種，予以出版，希望台灣菜作為一烹飪系統，得以確立，中國烹飪藝術更加進步。我們亦在此對味全文化教育基金會表示敬意。

- ●中央研究院院士
- ●國立台灣大學教授
- ●行政院文化建設委員會
　前主任委員

Foreword

The art of Chinese cooking is spreading throughout the world, as in recent decades, Chinese food has become ever more popular globally.

Although China is vast and plentiful, the population is great — making food shortages unavoidable. In order to deal with these shortages over thousands of years, Chinese have accumulated experience in developing methods of using elements to their maximum. Chinese know their natural surrounding, and how to get food from it, better than any other people. Additionally, they are able to completely utilize this to their benefit. For example, the use of animals is not limited to their meat, but extends to their organs. In terms of the uniqueness of Chinese food, a wealth of ingredients are used, creating a multitude of distinctive dishes. Menus at Chinese restaurants offer selections often two to three times as numerous as those offered at foreign restaurants. Perhaps this is a reason why Chinese food is so welcomed.

China consists of many regions, each having its own special foods. The more famous of these include: Beijing, Shantung Province, Szechuan Province, Hunan Province, Yangchow, Kiangsu-Chekiang, or Canton and Chaochu of Kwantung Province. Taiwanese cuisine is derived from the food system of Fukien Province — in particular, that of the city of Foochow, and Southern Fukien. However, Taiwan was occupied by the Japanese for half a century. After the recovery of Taiwan, by the Chinese, many people from all provinces of China immigrated to Taiwan. Society and all aspects of culture were greatly influenced due to these events; also due to these factors, Taiwanese cuisine, despite still being primarily Fukienese, has also incorporated the cooking techniques of all influences — creating a new cooking system.

The most outstanding features of Taiwanese foods are their clarity and lightness. Use of the knife is delicate and precise. Sweet and sour ingredients are used virtuously.

Ingredients, by means of soup, become winning dishes. Taiwan is an island with a rich variety of seafoods available to its people. This is why seafoods are predominant in Taiwanese cooking. Cooking methods, other than the traditional one of steaming, include: cooking, stewing (double boiling), frying, stir-frying, deep-frying, baking. We have also inherited, through the experience of Japanese cuisine, techniques in the preparation of raw and/or cold dishes. Lastly, the use of foods as supplemental curatives is an aspect of Taiwanese cooking. Foods, assisted by Chinese medicinal ingredients, are stewed in a steamer, and used to expel latent heat and/or "fire," as well as increase strength in the physical body. The methods and ingredients applied have enabled an expansion of Chinese traditional food curatives.

Wei-Chuan Cultural and Educational Foundation, by means of Taiwanese cuisine, has recorded a new system in the art of Chinese cooking. Recipes recorded in this cookbook include: twenty-six seafood, seventeen meat, six vegetable, seven egg and tofu, nine soup, eight snack, and five rice porridge — a total of seventy-eight.

By publishing this edition we hope that Taiwanese cuisine will attain recognition as a new system of cooking, while adding progress to the techniques of Chinese cooking. We would also at this time like to express our respect for the Wei-Chuan Cultural and Educational Foundation.

Dr. Chi-Lu Chen

- Member, Academia Sinica, R.O.C.
- Professor, National Taiwan University
- Former Chairman of the Chinese Cultural Development Council, Executive Yuan

前言

　　中國，地大物博，由於各地區生活習慣及出產作物的不同，發展出來的菜式也各具風貌。一般人到餐館，只知道菜名；但對於口味所代表的特色，大多未詳加研究。但「食」在生活中占著極重的份量，因此，認識各地菜餚也是對我國文化更深入的了解。

　　從今年開始，味全文教基金會將針對我國各地區的菜餚作有系統的研究並出版成書。而「台灣菜」即是我們的起步。近年來，台灣在國際經濟舞台上占有舉足輕重的地位，也因此國際人士對台灣菜漸漸發生興趣，這是基金會決定出版區域性食譜叢書時，以「台灣菜」打先鋒的主要因素。

　　早期的台灣百姓大多來自福建沿海，因此台灣菜的口味和福建菜頗爲相似。但由於台灣經過日本統治長達數十年之久，加上大陸淪陷後各省人士遷居來台，以致時下的台灣菜口味可說是綜合各省菜餚及日本菜的精華而自成一格。

　　在材料選擇上，由於台灣四周沿海，因此菜餚多以海鮮爲主。尤其受到海產養殖業發達的影響，台灣菜出現了許多精緻料理，例如九孔、蝦等。典型的台灣菜羹湯特多，所以有「台灣菜，湯湯水水」的說法，但是在口味方面，則偏重清鮮、淡雅。至於有些人以爲台灣菜多屬小吃，其實不然，只要溶入其中，台式宴會菜絕對上得了枱面。

　　出版「台灣菜」食譜，是味全文教基金會研究中國區域性菜餚的第一步。這本書得以順利出版，除了感謝味全家政班同仁不斷收集資料及研究製作外，還要特別謝謝味全家政班的黃德興老師及楊文典老師的精心烹調製作。

林麗華

Introduction

China is a fertile and immense country where each region's way of life, crops and products are different. Styles of cuisine developed in each region have their own practices. Most people going to a restaurant know only the name of a dish, but in regard to the individuality of taste which it represents the majority have limited knowledge. However, cuisine carries tremendous meaning in Chinese daily life, and it is for this reason, to understand each region's foods is also to have a greater understanding of Chinese culture.

Starting this year, Wei-Chuan Cultural and Educational Foundation will focus on each region of China's foods, and do a series of research and publications. "Chinese Cuisine—Taiwanese Style," is the beginning of this endeavor. Taiwan possesses a significant and important role in the international economic stage, and because of this, the international community is gradually discovering an interest in Taiwan's foods. This is also a reason why Wei-Chuan Cultural and Educational Foundation has decided to publish a series of regionally distinctive cookbooks, as well as the primary factor in using "Chinese Cuisine — Taiwanese Style" as a forerunner.

The earlier population of Taiwan came from along the coast of Fukien, so that the flavor of foods from both areas is somewhat similar. However, due to the several decades of Japanese reign of Taiwan, and the Communist takeover of Mainland China — which caused immigration to Taiwan from all provinces of China, over a length of time, the flavor of Taiwanese cuisine became a mixture of all province's and the essence of Japanese cuisine — becoming a standard in itself.

In the selection of ingredients, as Taiwan is surrounded by the ocean, seafoods are used extensively. Above all, the frequent use of seafoods has been influenced by the booming development of commercial breeding. In Taiwanese cuisine numerous exquisite foods appear. For example, abalone and shrimp. Typical of Taiwanese cuisine is the great number of soup stocks, resulting in it being referred to as a "soupy" cuisine. Taiwanese cuisine also places emphasis on lighter flavors and natural sweetness of foods. Some people believe that Taiwanese foods belong in the catagory of snacks. This is not true. Whenever attending a banquet, Taiwanese dishes are sure to be included in the menu.

The publishing of the "Chinese Cuisine — Taiwanese Style" cookbook is Wei-Chuan Cultural and Educational Foundation's first step in the research of regional cooking of China. I would like to thank, for the smooth completion of this publication, the members of the Wei-Chuan Cooking School, for their unfaltering collection of information and research, as well as Cooking School instructors — Mr. De-Shing Huang, and Mr. Wen-Dian Yang, for their devotion to cookery.

Lee Hwa Lin

清 粥

材料：

白米……………1 杯　　水……………6 杯

❶白米洗淨、瀝乾水分，加6杯水煮開，再以小火燜煮約15分鐘即可。

■加入已削皮切好的地瓜塊一起煮，即爲「地瓜粥」。

虱目魚粥

材料：

虱目魚中段　400公克
高湯……………6 杯
白飯……………2 杯
薑絲……………2 大匙
芹菜末………1 大匙

①｛ 鹽……………1 小匙
味精……$\frac{1}{8}$小匙
麻油、胡椒粉…
………各少許

❶虱目魚洗淨，切約1公分寬片狀，入開水略燙，撈起備用。

❷白飯2杯，入高湯6杯煮開，續入魚片，以小火燜煮10分鐘，再入①料拌勻，起鍋前灑上薑絲及芹菜末即可。

絲瓜粥

材料：

絲瓜 ………400公克
瘦豬肉……60公克
高湯……………6 杯
白飯……………2 杯
蝦米、油…各2 大匙

葱段……………6 段
①｛ 鹽……………1 小匙
味精……$\frac{1}{8}$小匙
胡椒粉…………少許

❶絲瓜去皮、洗淨，與瘦肉均切1公分寬薄片；蝦米洗淨、瀝乾備用。

❷鍋燒熱，入油2大匙，先入葱段爆香，續入蝦米及瘦肉拌炒數下，隨入絲瓜炒約5分鐘，入高湯6杯及白飯煮開，再入①料，以小火燜煮約10分鐘，關火，灑上胡椒粉即可。

桂圓糯米粥

材料：

水……………7 杯
圓糯米………1 杯
糖……………$\frac{3}{4}$ 杯

桂圓肉………$\frac{1}{2}$ 杯
酒……………1 大匙
桂花醬………$\frac{1}{2}$大匙

❶桂圓肉洗淨，瀝乾水分備用。

❷糯米洗淨瀝乾，入水7杯，以大火煮開，改小火燜煮10分鐘，拌入桂圓及糖，再燜煮約6〜7分鐘，入酒及桂花醬拌勻即可。

6 人份　Serves 6

Rice Porridge

INGREDIENTS:

| 1 c. | white rice |
| 6 c. | water |

❶ Rinse the rice until the water runs clear, then drain. Bring the rice and 6 cups of water to a boil, cover, and simmer for approximately 15 minutes.

■ Add cut pieces of peeled sweet potato and cook with rice to make "Sweet Potato Rice Porridge."

Milk Fish Rice Porridge

INGREDIENTS:

400 g. (14 oz.)	milk fish - center portion
6 c.	chicken broth
2 c.	white rice
2 T.	shredded ginger
1 T.	minced Chinese celery
① { 1 t.	salt.
Dash each:	sesame oil, pepper

❶ Cut fish into 1 cm. slices. Blanch.

❷ Bring the rice and chicken broth to a boil. Add fish, simmer for 10 minutes, stir in ① . Sprinkle on ginger and celery before serving.

Loofah Rice Porridge

INGREDIENTS:

400 g. (14 oz.)	loofah (sponge) gourd
60 g. (2 oz.)	lean pork
6 c.	chicken broth
2 c.	white rice
2 T. each:	small dried shrimp, oil
6 sections	green onion
Dash	pepper
①　1 t.	salt

❶ Peel the gourd. Cut gourd and pork into thin slices. Rinse the shrimp.

❷ Heat the wok and add 2 tablespoons oil. Fry the green onion until fragrance is emitted, then add the shrimp and pork. Stir-fry briefly. Add the gourd and fry for approximately 5 minutes. Add the soup broth and rice; bring this to a boil, add ① and simmer for about 10 minutes. Turn off the burner. Sprinkle on pepper just before serving.

Sweet Longan Rice Porridge

INGREDIENTS:

7 c.	water
1 c.	round glutinous rice
¾ c.	sugar
½ c.	seedless dried longan
1 T.	wine
½ T.	sweet osmanthus sauce

❶ Rinse, then drain the longans.

❷ Rinse the rice until the water runs clear, drain, add water, and bring to a boil over a high flame. Simmer for 10 minutes. Stir in the longans and sugar, then simmer for 6 - 7 more minutes. Add the wine and osmanthus sauce; stir until evenly mixed.

目錄

海鮮類 *Seafoods*

芝麻梅花蝦	Sesame Prawns	10
糖醋奶油抱	Sweet and Sour Buttered Firh Pookets	10
玉 蘭 干 貝	Magnolia Scallops	10
蔭 豉 鮮 蚵	Oysters with Black Bean Sauce	15
醬 油 魚 片	Soy Sauce Fish Fillet	16
糖 醋 魚 片	Sweet and Sour Fish Fillet	17
蛋 黃 中 卷	Yolk-Centered Squid Roll	18
鐵 板 花 枝 卷	Cuttlefish Rolls	20
三 絲 魚 卷	Colorful Fish Rolls	22
芙 蓉 魚 卷	Hibiscus Fish Rolls	22
韭 黃 蝦 卷	Chinese Chive Shrimp Rolls	22
香 菇 蝦 塔	Mushroom Shrimp Pagodas	22
玫 瑰 大 蝦	Rose Prawns	28
蜂 巢 蝦 窩	Honeycomb Shrimp	30
生 炒 蝦 鬆	Lettuce Rolled Shrimp	32
醬 肉 魚 丁	Meat Sauce Fish	34
銀 魚 花 生	Fish Peanuts	36
蠔 油 九 孔	Oyster Sauce Abalone	37
蒜 泥 九 孔	Garlic Purée Abalone	38
五 味 九 孔	Five Spice Abalone	40
沙 拉 九 孔	Abalone Salad	40
蒜 仁 田 腿	Garlic Frog Legs	41
芙 蓉 蟹	Smiling Crab	42
炒 豆 乳 蟹	Beancurd Crab	43
砂 鍋 粉 絲 蟹	Crab with Bean Thread Casserole	44
蟹 肉 黃 瓜	Cucumber Crab Rolls	46

肉 類 *Meats*

金 茸 肚 絲	Golden Mushroom with Pork Maw	48
桂 筍 肉 絲	Bamboo and Pork Julienne	48
蔭 豉 肉 丁	Pork with Black Beans	48
蜜 汁 溜 肉	Honey Glazed Pork	53
蒸 蛋 黃 肉	Sunshine Pork	54
燕 絲 肉 球	Shredded Pork Balls	55
油 條 雙 脆	Double Crispy Delight	56
西 芹 雞 片	Celery Chicken	58
雪 茸 雞 球	Snow Chicken Balls	58
葱 燒 去 骨 雞	Onion Chicken Fillet	58
杏 仁 雞 片	Almond Chicken Slices	63
鹽 酥 雞 塊	Flaky Chicken	64
腰 果 牛 鬆	Lettuce Cups with Beet & Cashews	65
葱 爆 牛 肉	Exploding Onion Beef	66
銀 芽 牛 肉	Silver Sprout Beef	66
韭 黃 牛 肉	Beef and Yellow Chinese Chives	66
干 煎 牛 排	Sautéed Steak	71

Contents

蔬菜類 *Vegetables*

冬 菇 芥 菜	Mushrooms and Mustard Greens ··· 72
韮黃炒四絲	Chives and Friends ················ 72
扁 魚 白 菜	Fish-flavoved Cabbage ·············· 72
奶 油 白 菜	Creamed Cabbage ················· 77
髮 菜 豆 苗	Black Moss and Pea Leaves ········ 78
澎 湖 絲 瓜	Fragrant Loofah ·················· 79

蛋、豆腐類 *Eggs & Beancurd*

煎 菜 脯 蛋	Radish and Egg Pancake ··········· 80
富 貴 銀 耳	Precious White Fungus ············· 82
蟳 焗 豆 腐	Baked Crab Sauce Tofu·············· 84
鐵 板 豆 腐	Fondue Tofu ····················· 84
家 鄉 豆 腐	Home-Style Tofu···················· 84
炸 豆 腐	Fried Tofu ······················ 89
干 煎 豆 腐	Sautéed Bean Curd ············· 90

湯 類 *Soups*

金 針 雞 湯	Lily Bud Chicken Soup ············· 91
一 品 燉 雞	First-Class Stewed Chicken Soup ··· 92
蛋 衣 蝦 卷	Egg-Dressed Shrimp Rolls ··········· 94
螺 肉 蒜 湯	Garlic Escargot' Fondue·············· 96
蛤 蜊 冬 瓜 濃	Clam and Winter Melon Soup ····· 98
番 茄 排 骨 湯	Tomato and Pork Rib Soup········ 100
髮 菜 濃 湯	Forest Soup ····················· 101
雞 絲 濃 湯	Chicken Julienne Soup ·········· 102
花 瓜 雞 湯	Pickled Cucumber Chicken Soup·· 103

點心類 *Snacks*

筒 仔 米 糕	Bamboo Cup Rice Pudding········· 104
粽 子	Jungdz····················· 104
蚵 仔 麵 線	Oyster Noodle Strings ·············· 104
蚵 仔 煎	Oyster Pan Fritters ············· 109
八 寶 糯 米 卷	Eight Treasure Glutinous Rice Rolls ·· 110
香 酥 雞 卷	Fragrant Bean Curd Skin Roll ······ 112
魷 魚 羹	Broth of Squid Soup················ 114
香 菇 赤 肉 羹	Black Mushroom and Pork Soup··· 116

承蒙台灣凱斯股份有限公司、曉芳陶藝有限公司、集緻精品等提供道具，謹此致謝。

Many thanks to K's Collection, Taiwan Co., Ltd., Hsiao Fang Pottery Arts Co., Ltd., and Joina Arts, for providing settings for the photographs.

芝麻梅花蝦：作法見第12頁
糖醋奶油抱：作法見第13頁
玉 蘭 干 貝：作法見第14頁

Sesame Prawns (p.12)
Sweet and Sour Buttered Fish Pockets (p.13)
Magnolia Scallops (p.14)

芝麻梅花蝦

Sesame Prawns

材料：

明蝦或大草蝦	………………	12隻
冬粉	………………	1把
油	………………	4杯
熟白芝麻	………………	3大匙

①	太白粉	…………………	$\frac{3}{4}$杯
	麵粉	…………………	$\frac{1}{4}$杯
②	高湯	…………………	$\frac{1}{2}$杯
	蕃茄醬	………………	$1\frac{1}{2}$大匙
	糖、白醋	……………	各2小匙
	鹽	…………………	$\frac{1}{8}$小匙
③	蛋白	…………………	$\frac{1}{3}$個
	太白粉	………………	1大匙
	酒、麻油	……………	各1小匙
	糖	…………………	$\frac{1}{2}$小匙
	鹽	…………………	$\frac{1}{4}$小匙
	味精、胡椒粉	………	各$\frac{1}{8}$小匙

❶蝦去頭、去殼、留尾（圖1），去腸泥，洗淨瀝乾，片開背部（勿斷），再將中間劃一刀（圖2），入③料拌醃數分鐘，取出，將蝦尾部自中間劃刀部分，由腹部往背部穿上來（圖3），沾上①料備用。

❷將油燒至7分熱（約140℃，280°F），入冬粉炸至膨脹，撈起瀝油，排盤墊底。將火關小，待油溫降至6分熱（120℃，240°F），再開大火，入蝦炸熟，撈起瀝油備用。

❸②料煮開，淋在蝦上，再將蝦排在冬粉上，灑上熟白芝麻即可。

INGREDIENTS:

	12	jumbo prawns or shrimp
	1 bunch (1⅓ oz.)	bean thread noodles
	4 c.	oil
	3 T.	cooked white sesame seeds
①	¾ c.	cornstarch
	¼ c.	flour
②	½ c.	chicken broth
	1½ T.	ketchup
	2 t. each:	sugar, white vinegar
	⅛ t.	salt
③	⅓	egg white
	1 T.	cornstarch
	1 t. each:	wine, sesame oil
	½ t.	sugar
	¼ t.	salt
	⅛ t.	pepper

❶ Remove the head and shell from prawn leaving the tail (illus. 1). Devein, rinse and drain the prawns before making a shallow lengthwise cut along the back of each; make one slit in the middle (illus. 2). Marinate the prawns in ③ for several minutes. Bring the tail down and through the middle slit (illus. 3). Coat the prawns with ① .

❷ Heat oil to 140° C (280° F). Fry bean threads until they are puffy and expanded, then drain. Place bean threads on serving platter. Turn burner down to low flame and wait until oil reaches a temperature of 120° C (240° F), then turn the flame high. Deep fry prawns until done, then drain.

❸ Place ② in wok and bring to a boil. Pour this onto prawns. Prawns and sauce are then placed on bean threads. Sprinkle sesame seeds on the very top.

■ Please note that Taiwanese use rice wine as a cooking wine. Rice wine is similar in flavor to a dry white grape wine.

12人份　Serves 12

糖醋奶油抱

Sweet and Sour Buttered Fish Pockets

材料：

魚肉	480公克
洋葱末	120公克
絞肉	40公克
香菇末	20公克
奶油	3大匙
高麗菜	3片

① 薑汁、酒……各1小匙
　 鹽……¼小匙
　 味精……⅛小匙

② 薑汁、酒……各1小匙
　 糖……½小匙
　 鹽……¼小匙
　 味精……⅛小匙

③ 高湯……¾杯
　 蕃茄醬……2大匙
　 糖……1大匙
　 白醋……2小匙
　 鹽……¼小匙

④ 太白粉、水……各½大匙
麻油……1小匙

❶將魚肉洗淨，切0.5×4×5公分連刀片（圖1）12片，入①料拌勻備用。

❷鍋燒熱，入奶油3大匙，續入洋葱、絞肉、香菇末爆香，再入②料拌勻，放入冰箱冰涼爲餡備用。

❸將餡取出分成12等份，每份餡塞入魚片內（圖2），開口處包好壓緊，共12份備用。

❹烤箱預熱至300℃（600℉），烤盤上墊高麗菜葉，再將魚片置其上（圖3），入烤箱烤4～5分鐘，取出備用。

❺③料煮開，以④料勾芡，灑上麻油，淋在魚片上即可。

■免魚、草魚、黃魚等肉質多的魚均可。

INGREDIENTS:

480 g. (1 lb. 1 oz.)	fish fillet
120 g. (¼ lb.)	minced onion
40 g. (1⅓ oz.)	ground pork
20 g. (⅔ oz.)	minced, soaked black mushroom
3 T.	butter
3 leaves	cabbage

① 1 t. each: ginger juice, wine
　 ¼ t. salt

② 1 t. each: ginger juice, wine
　 ½ t. sugar
　 ¼ t. salt

③ ¾ c. chicken broth
　 2 T. ketchup
　 1 T. sugar
　 2 t. white vinegar
　 ¼ t. salt

④ ½ T. each: cornstarch, water
1 t. sesame oil

❶ Rinse the fish clean and cut into 12, 0.5×4×5 cm. slices. Cut each slice down the middle but not through (illus. 1). Coat with ① .

❷ Heat the wok and add 3 tablespoons butter. Sauté the onion, ground pork and mushrooms until fragrant, then stir fry in ② . Place in the refrigerator to cool. This is the filling.

❸ Divide the filling into 12 portions. Place a portion in each fish slice (illus. 2). Close the top opening tightly.

❹ Heat the oven to 300° C. (600° F). Use a heatproof dish to place the cabbage in, then place fish on top of the cabbage (illus. 3). Bake for 4-5 minutes. Remove from oven.

❺ Bring ③ to a boil, then stir in ④ to thicken. Sprinkle on sesame oil. Pour this sauce on the fish and serve.

■ Any meaty fish may be used.

13

玉蘭干貝

Magnolia Scallops

材料：

花枝肉	⋯⋯⋯⋯⋯⋯	300公克
絞肥肉	⋯⋯⋯⋯⋯⋯	40公克
干貝	⋯⋯⋯⋯⋯⋯	6個
大白菜	⋯⋯⋯⋯⋯⋯	8片
竹簾	⋯⋯⋯⋯⋯⋯	1個

① 蛋白 ⋯⋯⋯⋯⋯⋯ $\frac{1}{2}$個
　酒 ⋯⋯⋯⋯⋯⋯ 1小匙
　鹽 ⋯⋯⋯⋯⋯⋯ $\frac{3}{8}$小匙
　味精 ⋯⋯⋯⋯⋯⋯ $\frac{1}{8}$小匙

② 高湯 ⋯⋯⋯⋯⋯⋯ $\frac{1}{2}$杯
　蒸干貝汁 ⋯⋯⋯⋯⋯⋯ $\frac{1}{4}$杯
　酒 ⋯⋯⋯⋯⋯⋯ $\frac{1}{2}$大匙
　鹽 ⋯⋯⋯⋯⋯⋯ $\frac{1}{4}$小匙
　胡椒粉 ⋯⋯⋯⋯⋯⋯ 少許

③ 太白粉、水 ⋯⋯⋯⋯⋯⋯ 各$\frac{1}{2}$大匙
麻油 ⋯⋯⋯⋯⋯⋯ 少許

❶花枝去皮、去腸泥、洗淨，以肉捶捶成花枝漿，拌入①料及絞肥肉，甩打數下，分成2等份備用。

❷干貝洗淨，加水$\frac{1}{2}$杯入蒸籠蒸軟，撕成絲，蒸汁留作②料；大白菜洗淨，燙軟漂涼備用。

❸竹簾上擺4片白菜葉，兩片兩片頭尾相反間插排列（圖1）；取一份餡置其上，包捲成長條狀（圖2），共做2份；再切3公分長段備用。

❹將白菜卷兩頭沾上干貝絲（圖3），置盤排好，入蒸籠，大火蒸5分鐘，取出白菜卷，湯汁留著備用。

❺②料及❹之湯汁煮開，入③料勾芡，灑上麻油，再淋於白菜卷即可。

INGREDIENTS:

300 g. (⅔ lb.)		squid
40 g. (1⅓ oz.)		fatty ground pork
6		dried scallops
8 leaves		nappa cabbage
1		bamboo mat
①	½	egg white
	1 t.	wine
	⅜ t.	salt
②	½ c.	chicken broth
	¼ c.	juice from steaming scallops
	½ T.	wine
	¼ t.	salt
	Dash	pepper
③	½ T. each:	cornstarch, water
Dash		sesame oil

❶ Remove the skin and organs from the squid. Rinse clean, pound into a mash, then mix with ① and ground pork. Mix several times by scooping out mixture with hand and throwing back into bowl. Divide into 2 equal portions.

❷ Rinse the scallops clean. Place ½ cup water in steamer and steam scallops until soft. Shred the scallops. Retain the juice from steaming for use in ② . Wash, parboil, and cool the cabbage.

❸ Place 4 cabbage leaves on the bamboo mat, alternating leaves and stems at top (illus. 1). Place one filling on top and roll into a cylinder (illus. 2). Make 2. Cut rolls into 3 cm. wide sections.

❹ Dip both sides of the cabbage sections in the scallop shreds (illus. 3). Place on plate and steam over a high flame for 5 minutes. Remove cabbage sections to platter. Retain juice for use in step ❺ .

❺ Bring retained juice from step ❹ and ② to a boil. Thicken with ③ , then sprinkle on sesame oil. Pour this mixture on cabbage rolls.

蔭豉鮮蚵

Oysters with Black Bean Sauce

材料：

生蚵 ⋯⋯⋯⋯400公克	醬油膏⋯⋯⋯ 3 大匙
蒜苗⋯⋯⋯⋯80公克	黑豆豉⋯⋯⋯ 2 大匙
油⋯⋯⋯⋯⋯ 3 大匙	② 酒⋯⋯⋯⋯ 1 大匙

① 薑片(指甲片)、紅辣
椒片⋯⋯⋯各 1 大匙
蒜片、葱末
⋯⋯⋯⋯各 1 小匙

糖⋯⋯⋯⋯⋯ $\frac{1}{2}$ 小匙
味精⋯⋯⋯⋯ $\frac{1}{4}$ 小匙
麻油⋯⋯⋯⋯ 1 小匙
太白粉、鹽⋯⋯⋯少許

❶生蚵先用太白粉、鹽洗淨(圖1)，瀝乾水分，入70
　℃熱水中燙至水開(圖2)，隨即關火；燜一下，撈
　起，再以清水洗淨，瀝乾備用。
❷蒜苗切丁狀(圖3)備用。
❸油鍋燒熱，入油3大匙，續入①料爆香，再入②料
　煮開，最後入鮮蚵拌勻，起鍋前灑上麻油、蒜苗即
　可。
■黑豆豉處理法：
　黑豆豉先洗淨、瀝乾水分；再以薑片3片、酒2大
　匙、味精 $\frac{1}{4}$ 小匙醃泡15分鐘入味，取出黑豆豉，瀝
　乾備用。

INGREDIENTS:

400 g. (14 oz.)		oysters
80 g. (2¾ oz.)		leeks
3 T.		oil
①	1 T. each:	sliced-(fingernail-sized) ginger, red chili pepper
	1 t. each:	minced-green onion, garlic
②	3 T.	thick soy sauce
	2 T.	(fermented) black beans
	1 T.	wine
	½ t.	sugar
1 t.		sesame oil
Dash each:		cornstarch, salt

❶ Use the cornstarch and salt to clean the oysters (illus. 1). Remove and drain. Place in 70° C (140° F) water. When the water comes to a boil (illus. 2), turn off the burner and let sit. Remove the oysters almost immediately, then rinse and drain.

❷ Cut the leeks into pieces (illus. 3).

❸ Heat the wok and add 3 tablespoons of oil. Add ① and stir fry until fragrant. Add ② and bring to a boil, then stir in oysters. Sprinkle on sesame oil and leeks, then remove to serving platter.

■ Method for preparing black beans:
Rinse the black beans clean, then drain. Marinate in 3 slices of ginger and 2 tablespoons of wine 15 minutes for flavoring. Remove and drain to be used.

6人份　Serves 6

醬油魚片

Soy Sauce Fish Fillet

材料：
免魚肉 ························300公克
油 ···························· 3 杯

① | 葱段 ····················· 6 段
　| 薑絲 ····················· 1 大匙
　| 紅辣椒絲 ················· 1 小匙

② | 蛋白 ·····················½ 個
　| 酒、醬油 ··············各 1 大匙
　| 太白粉 ···················½ 大匙
　| 味精 ·····················¼ 小匙

③ | 醬油膏 ··················· 2 大匙
　| 酒 ······················· 1 小匙
　| 糖 ·······················½ 小匙
　| 味精 ····················· 少許
麻油 ······················· 少許

❶免魚肉切3×5×0.2公分薄片(圖1)，入②料醃數分
　鐘備用。
❷鍋燒熱，入油3杯，熱至120℃(240°F)，入免魚肉過
　油(圖2)，隨即撈起瀝油備用。
❸鍋內留油2大匙，入①料爆香，隨入③料及魚片(
　圖3)拌勻，起鍋前灑上麻油即可。

INGREDIENTS:
300 g. (⅔ lb.)　　fish fillets
3 c.　　　　　　　oil

① | 6 sections　　green onion
　| 1 T.　　　　 shredded ginger
　| 1 t.　　　　 shredded red chili
　|　　　　　　　　pepper

② | ½　　　　　　 egg white
　| 1 T. each:　 wine, soy sauce
　| ½ T.　　　　 cornstarch

③ | 2 T.　　　　 thick soy sauce
　| 1 t.　　　　 wine
　| ½ t.　　　　 sugar
Dash　　　　　　sesame oil

❶ Cut the fish into thin slices of 3×5×0.2 cm.
(illus. 1). Marinate fish in ② for several
minutes.

❷ Heat the wok and add 3 cups oil. When
wok reaches temperature of 120° C
(240° F), pass the fish through the oil to
precook (illus. 2). Remove and drain.

❸ Retain 2 tablespoons of oil in the wok and
add ① . When ① becomes fragrant add
③ , then fish (illus. 3), stir-frying evenly.
Sprinkle on sesame oil just before removing from wok.

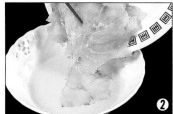

6人份　Serves 6

糖醋魚片

Sweet and Sour Fish Fillet

材料：

魚肉 ……………160公克		
油…………………… 4 杯		
①	洋葱絲………80公克	
	葱段……………¼ 杯	
	薑絲、辣椒絲………	
	……………各 5 公克	
②	蛋………………… 1 個	
	麵粉………… 3 大匙	
	白醬油………½ 大匙	
	蒜末………… 1 小匙	
	味精…………¼ 小匙	

③	高湯……………¾ 杯	
	蕃茄醬……… 2 大匙	
	糖………… 3 小匙	
	黑醋、白醋各 1 小匙	
	鹽…………¼ 小匙	
	味精…………⅛ 小匙	
④	太白粉、水…………	
	………各 1½ 小匙	
麻油………… 1 小匙		

❶魚肉切薄片(圖1)，入②料拌勻(圖2)備用。

❷將油燒至8分熱(約160°C，320°F)，入魚片炸至金黃色(圖3)，撈起瀝油，置於盤中備用。

❸鍋內留油3大匙，入①料爆香，續入③料煮開，以④料勾芡，起鍋前灑上麻油，並淋在魚片上即可。

INGREDIENTS:

160 g. (5½ oz.)		fish fillet
4 c.		oil
①	80 g. (2¾ oz.)	julienned onion
	¼ c.	green onion sections
	5 g. (⅙ oz.) each:	shredded - ginger, red chili pepper
②	1	egg
	3 T.	flour
	½ T.	light soy sauce
	1 t.	minced garlic
③	¾ c.	chicken broth
	2 T.	ketchup
	3 t.	sugar
	1 t. each:	dark vinegar, white vinegar
	¼ t.	salt
④	1½ t. each:	cornstarch, water
	1 t.	sesame oil

❶ Cut the fish into thin slices (illus. 1). Coat the fish with ② (illus. 2).

❷ Heat oil to 160° C (320° F). Fry fish until golden brown (illus. 3). Remove and drain, then place in middle of platter.

❸ Retain 3 tablespoons oil in wok. Fry ① until it emits fragrance. Add ③, and when it boils, stir in ④ to thicken. Before removing from wok, sprinkle on sesame oil. Pour sauce on top of fish.

17

蛋黃中卷

Yolk-Centered Squid Roll

材料：

透抽 ……………400公克（約2隻）
生鹹蛋黃 ………………… 6個
罐頭青豆仁、火腿 ………各70公克
① ┌ 酒 …………………………1大匙
  │ 味精、糖 …………各 $\frac{1}{4}$ 小匙
  └ 胡椒粉 ………………………少許
沙拉醬 …………………………2大匙

❶透抽去皮及頭，切去尾部一小部分（圖1），
　去腸泥，洗淨備用。
❷蛋黃切小丁、火腿亦切小丁，與青豆仁及①
　料拌勻為餡備用。
❸取適量的餡塞入透抽內，塞緊後頭部以牙籤
　固定（圖2），另以牙籤將身體部分穿數個洞
　（圖3）透氣備用。
❹蒸籠的水燒開，將透抽放入蒸籠，大火蒸約
　12分鐘，取出待涼，切約1公分片狀排盤。
❺食時沾沙拉醬即可。

INGREDIENTS:

2-200 g. (7 oz.) each:	squid
70 g. (2½ oz.) each:	ham, canned soy beans
6	raw salt-preserved egg yolks
① ⎰ 1 T.	wine
⎱ ¼ t.	sugar
Dash	pepper
2 T.	mayonnaise or salad dressing

❶ Remove heads and skins from the squid. Cut off a small portion of the tails (illus. 1), and remove organs. Rinse clean.

❷ Cut the egg yolk into small pieces, then ham. Mix them evenly with the soy beans and ① . This is the filling.

❸ Stuff the squids with a suitable amount of filling. Use toothpicks to stablize the backs (illus. 2). Use a toothpick to make several holes in the bodies, to let out steam when cooking (illus. 3).

❹ When the water in the steamer boils, place the squid in, and over a high flame steam for 12 minutes. Remove and cool. Cut into 1 cm. wide slices and arrange on a serving platter.

❺ Mayonnaise or salad dressing is used as a dip when serving.

6人份　Serves 6

鐵板花枝卷　Cuttlefish Rolls

<table>
<tr><td>材料：</td><td></td><td>INGREDIENTS:</td><td></td></tr>
<tr><td>花枝</td><td>300公克</td><td>300 g. (²⁄₃ lb.)</td><td>cuttlefish</td></tr>
<tr><td>洋火腿</td><td>80公克</td><td>80 g. (2¾ oz.)</td><td>ham</td></tr>
<tr><td>肥肉</td><td>60公克</td><td>60 g. (2 oz.)</td><td>fatty pork</td></tr>
<tr><td>香菜末</td><td>½ 杯</td><td>½ c.</td><td>minced coriander</td></tr>
<tr><td>太白粉</td><td>4 大匙</td><td>4 T.</td><td>cornstarch</td></tr>
<tr><td>豆皮</td><td>2 張</td><td>2</td><td>bean curd sheets</td></tr>
<tr><td>紫菜皮</td><td>1 張</td><td>1</td><td>laver seaweed sheet ("nori")</td></tr>
<tr><td>蒜苗</td><td>2 支</td><td>2 stems</td><td>leeks</td></tr>
<tr><td>油</td><td>4 杯</td><td>4 c.</td><td>oil</td></tr>
</table>

① 蛋白 ½ 個 — ½ egg white
麻油、熟白芝麻 各 1 大匙 — 1 T. each: sesame oil, cooked white sesame seeds
太白粉 ½ 大匙 — ½ T. cornstarch
鹽 ½ 小匙 — ½ t. salt
味精、胡椒粉 各少許 — Dash pepper

② 麵粉 2 大匙 — 2 T. flour
水 ½ 大匙 — ½ T. water

❶ 花枝洗淨，去頭及外皮，切開花枝，再切寬4公分長條片狀(圖1)，再拌入①料。②料拌勻是爲麵糊；均備用。

❷ 紫菜皮切成4份。洋火腿、肥肉切與紫菜同大小之薄片備用。

❸ 蒜苗切斜薄片，令蒜苗呈鬆散狀(圖2)，再與香菜末充份拌勻備用。

❹ 每張豆皮上，依次置肥肉片、花枝片、紫菜皮、火腿片、蒜苗、香菜末(圖3)、紫菜皮、花枝片、肥肉片、火腿片，包捲成扁平條狀，封口以麵糊黏合，即爲花枝卷。

❺ 將花枝卷沾裹太白粉，入5分熱（100℃，200℉)油鍋，大火炸至金黃色，撈起瀝油，切片排盤即可。

■ 食時可沾蕃茄醬。

❶ Rinse the cuttlefish clean. Remove head and outer skin. Butterfly, then cut into 4 cm. wide strips (illus. 1). Mix with ① . Mix ② evenly as a paste.

❷ Cut seaweed sheet into 4 sections. Cut ham and fatty pork into thin slices the same size as the cut seaweed sections.

❸ Cut the leeks into diagonal thin slices. Separate the leek slices into loose rings (illus. 2), then mix thoroughly with the coriander.

❹ Place in order on each bean curd sheet: pork, cuttlefish, seaweed, ham, the leeks and minced coriander (illus. 3), and once again, seaweed, cuttlefish, pork, and ham. Roll into a flat cylinder and seal with the paste. This is the squid roll.

❺ Coat the cuttlefish roll in cornstarch, then place in 100° C (200° F) oil; continue to deep fry, over a high flame, until golden brown, then remove and drain. Cut into slices and place on serving platter.

■ Ketchup may be used as a dip.

6人份　Serves 6

❶　❷　❸

三絲魚卷：作法見第24頁
芙蓉魚卷：作法見第25頁
韭黃蝦卷：作法見第26頁
香菇蝦塔：作法見第27頁

Colorful Fish Rolls (p.24)
Hibiscus Fish Rolls (p.25)
Chinese Chive Shrimp Rolls (P.26)
Mushroom Shrimp Pagodas (p.27)

三絲魚卷

Colorful Fish Rolls

材料：

冤魚肉	························300公克
油	························ 3 大匙
①	絞五花肉 ···············160公克
	魚漿、紅蘿蔔末······各60公克
	荸薺末···············40公克
	葱末···············3 大匙
②	香菇絲、薑絲、葱絲···各 2 大匙
	紅辣椒絲···············1 大匙
③	酒、麻油···············各½大匙
	鹽···············⅓小匙
	味精、胡椒粉···········各⅛小匙
④	高湯···············1 杯
	酒···············½大匙
	糖、鹽···············各⅓小匙
	味精、胡椒粉···········各⅛小匙
⑤	太白粉、水···········各 2 小匙

❶冤魚肉洗淨、切6×3×0.2公分薄片（圖1）；①料與③料拌勻（圖2）爲餡備用。

❷每一魚片各包入 1 大匙內餡，包捲成長條狀（圖3）。蒸籠的水燒開，再將魚卷放入蒸籠，大火蒸5～6分鐘，取出排盤備用。

❸鍋燒熱，入油3大匙，續入②料爆香，再入④料煮開，以⑤料勾芡，並淋在魚卷上即可。

INGREDIENTS:

300 g. (⅔ lb.)	fish fillet
3 T.	oil
①	160 g. (5½ oz.)	ground fatty pork
	60 g. (2 oz.) each:	mashed fish, minced carrot
	40 g. (1⅓ oz.)	minced water chestnut
	3 T.	minced green onion
②	2 T. each:	julienned - soaked black mushroom, ginger, green onion
	1 T.	julienned red chili pepper
③	½ T. each:	wine, sesame oil
	⅓ t.	salt
	⅛ t.	pepper
④	1 c.	chicken broth
	½ T.	wine
	⅓ t. each:	sugar, salt
	⅛ t.	pepper
⑤	2 t. each:	cornstarch, water

❶ Rinse the fish clean and cut into thin slices of 6×3×0.2 cms. (illus. 1). Mix ① and ③ together (illus. 2), as a filling.

❷ Place 1 tablespoon filling on each fish slice and roll to form a long cylinder (illus. 3). When the water in the steamer comes to a boil, place the fish in the steamer basket, and steam over a high flame for 5-6 minutes. Remove for later use.

❸ Heat the wok and add 3 tablespoons of oil. Fry ② until fragrant, then add ④ and bring to a boil. Stir in ⑤ to thicken. Pour this sauce on the fish rolls and serve.

6 人份　Serves 6

芙蓉魚卷

Hibiscus Fish Rolls

材料：

| 免魚肉 | …………………300公克 |
| 蛋白 | ……………………… 5 個 |

① 熟筍絲 ……………120公克
五花肉絲、紅蘿蔔絲…各80公克
香菇絲 ………………50公克
薑絲、葱絲…………各 1 大匙

② 麻油、太白粉………各 1 大匙
酒 …………………… 1 小匙
味精、鹽……………各 ¼ 小匙

③ 高湯 …………………1½ 杯
酒 …………………… 1 小匙
鹽 …………………… ½ 小匙
味精 ………………… ⅛ 小匙

④ 高湯…………………1½ 杯
鹽 …………………… ⅓ 小匙
味精 ………………… ⅛ 小匙
胡椒粉………………… 少許

⑤ 太白粉、水…………各 ½ 大匙
蛋黃 …………………… 3 個
雞油或麻油………………… 少許

❶免魚肉洗淨、切8×6公分薄片12片；①料與②料拌
　勻成餡，分成12份備用。
❷每一魚片各包 1 份內餡，包捲成長條狀。蒸籠鍋內
　水燒開，放入魚卷，大火蒸 5 分鐘，取出備用。
❸蛋白打散，與③料拌勻，以篩網過篩(圖 1)，放入
　深盤內，入蒸籠以小火蒸 10 分鐘取出，上置魚卷(
　圖 2)備用。
❹④料煮開，以⑤料勾芡，再拌入打散之蛋黃液（圖
　3)，起鍋前灑上雞油(或麻油)，並淋在魚卷即可。

INGREDIENTS:

300 g. (⅔ lb.)		fish fillet
5		egg whites
①	120 g. (¼ lb.)	julienned, canned bamboo shoots
	80 g. (2¾ oz.) each:	julienned - uncured bacon meat, carrot
	50 g. (1¾ oz.)	julienned, soaked black mushrooms
	1 T. each:	julienned - ginger, green onion
②	1 T. each:	sesame oil, cornstarch
	1 t.	wine
	¼ t.	salt
③	1½ c.	chicken broth
	1 t.	wine
	½ t.	salt
④	1½ c.	chicken broth
	⅓ t.	salt
	Dash	pepper
⑤	½ T. each:	cornstarch, water
3		egg yolks
Dash		chicken fat, or sesame oil

❶ Rinse the fish clean and cut into 12 thin slices of 8×6 cms. Mix ① and ② together, as a filling, then divide into 12 portions.

❷ Place one portion of filling on each fish slice and roll into a long cylinder. When the water in the steamer comes to a boil, place the fish in and steam for 5 minutes over a high flame. Remove for later use.

❸ Beat the egg whites, then stir in ③ . Pour through a strainer (illus. 1). Place in a deep heatproof dish, and steam for 10 minutes over a low flame. Remove, and place the fish rolls on top (illus. 2).

❹ Bring ④ to a boil, then stir in ⑤ to thicken; beat the egg yolks and stir in (illus. 3). Sprinkle on chicken fat (or sesame oil), then pour this sauce on the fish rolls and serve.

25

①

②

③

6 人份　Serves 6

韭黃蝦卷

Chinese Chive Shrimp Rolls

材料：

蘆蝦仁	150公克
韭黃	75公克
絞五花肉	45公克
荸薺	30公克
香菇	10公克
豆皮	3 張
油	4 杯

①
- 蛋白 …………………… ½ 個
- 鹽、味精 …………… 各 ¼ 小匙
- 胡椒粉 …………………… 少許

②
- 高湯 …………………… 2 大匙
- 麻油 …………………… ½ 大匙
- 糖、酒 …………… 各 ½ 小匙
- 胡椒粉 …………………… ⅛ 小匙

③ 太白粉、水 ………… 各 ½ 大匙

❶蝦仁去腸泥、洗淨，瀝乾水分；以刀背拍碎（圖1），並拌入①料備用。

❷韭黃洗淨切末；荸薺切末；香菇泡軟、去蒂切末；豆皮每張各切成4份（圖2）備用。

❸鍋燒熱，入油2大匙，再入絞肉炒香，續入香菇、韭黃、荸薺、蝦泥及②料拌勻，最後入③料勾芡，即爲內餡，盛盤待涼，分成12份備用。

❹每份豆皮上，各置1份內餡，包捲成長條狀（圖3），入5分熱(100°C，200°F)油鍋，大火炸至金黃色，撈起瀝油即可。

INGREDIENTS:

150 g. (⅓ lb.)	medium-sized shrimp or prawns
75 g. (2½ oz.)	yellow Chinese chives
45 g. (1½ oz.)	ground pork
30 g. (1 oz.)	water chestnuts
10 g. (⅓ oz.)	black dried mushrooms
3 sheets	bean curd skins
4 c.	oil

①
- ½ — egg white
- ¼ t. — salt
- Dash — pepper

②
- 2 T. — chicken broth
- ½ T. — sesame oil
- ½ t. each: — sugar, wine
- ⅛ t. — pepper

③ ½ T. each: — cornstarch, water

❶ Devein, rinse and drain shrimp. Use the side of the knife to break into pieces (illus. 1). Mix with ① .

❷ Clean and mince the yellow chives. Mince the water chestnuts. Soak the mushrooms until soft, then remove stems and mince. Cut each sheet of bean curd skin into 4 (illus. 2).

❸ Heat the wok and add 2 tablespoons oil. Stir fry the ground pork until fragrant, then add mushrooms, chives, chestnuts, shrimp and ② , mixing evenly. Lastly, thicken with ③ . This is the filling. Remove to platter. Cool, and divide into 12.

❹ Place one portion of filling on each bean sheet section. Roll (illus. 3). Place in 100° C (200° F) oil. Fry over a high flame until golden brown. Remove and drain.

香菇蝦塔

Mushroom Shrimp Pagodas

材料：

蝦仁	240公克
絞肥肉	40公克
荸薺末	40公克
香菇	12朵
太白粉	$\frac{1}{2}$ 杯
油	6 杯

①	蛋白	$\frac{1}{2}$ 個
	葱末、太白粉	各 $\frac{1}{2}$ 大匙
	薑汁、酒、麻油	各 1 小匙
	鹽、糖	各 $\frac{1}{4}$ 小匙
	胡椒粉	$\frac{1}{8}$ 小匙
	味精	少許
②	葱段	6 段
	薑片	2 片
	高湯	1 杯
	醬油	2 大匙
	麻油	1 大匙
	糖	1 小匙

❶蝦仁去腸泥、洗淨，瀝乾水分，以刀背拍碎；再與絞肥肉、荸薺末及①料拌勻成餡，分成12份（圖 1 ）備用。

❷香菇泡軟、去蒂、洗淨，入②料中；先以大火煮開再改小火煮5～6分鐘，取出瀝乾水分，上灑少許太白粉（圖 2 ）備用。

❸每一朵香菇，上置 1 份餡即為香菇塔（圖3），先蒸熟(約7～8分鐘)，再沾裹太白粉，續入 7 分熱（約140°C，280°F)油鍋，炸至金黃色，撈起瀝油即可。

■食時可沾蕃茄醬。

INGREDIENTS:

240 g. (8½ oz.)	shelled shrimp or prawns
40 g. (1⅓ oz.)	ground fatty meat
40 g. (1⅓ oz.)	minced water chestnuts
12	dried black mushrooms
½ c.	cornstarch
6 c.	oil

①	½	egg white
	½ T. each:	minced green onion, cornstarch
	1 t. each	ginger juice, wine, sesame oil
	¼ t. each:	salt, sugar
	⅛ t.	pepper
②	6 sections	green onion
	2 slices	ginger
	1 c.	chicken broth
	2 T.	soy sauce
	1 T.	sesame oil
	1 t.	sugar

❶ Devein the shrimp, rinse and drain. Use the side of the knife to break shrimp into pieces, then mix thoroughly the shrimp, ground fatty meat, water chestnuts, and ① . This is the filling. Divide into 12 portions (illus. 1).

❷ Soak mushrooms until soft, remove stems, then mix with ② . Bring this to a boil, then simmer for 5-6 minutes. Remove and drain the mushrooms, then coat with a small amount of cornstarch (illus. 2).

❸ Place on each mushroom one portion of filling, making a "pagoda" (illus. 3). Steam about 7 to 8 minutes then coat with cornstarch. Fry in 140° C (280° F) oil until golden brown. Remove and drain.

■ Ketchup may be used as a dip.

玫瑰大蝦　　Rose Prawns

材料：

大明蝦 ················6尾
肥豬肉··············60公克
紫菜皮 ···············2張
蛋 ···················2個
萵苣、紅蘿蔔片、火腿片 ··········
········ 各6片（4×9公分）
油 ···················4杯

①
| 蛋白 ·················1個 |
| 太白粉 ···············3大匙 |
| 酒、糖、麻油 ·········各1小匙 |
| 鹽、味精、胡椒粉······各½小匙 |

②
| 太白粉 ···············1杯 |
| 麵粉 ·················⅓杯 |

❶大明蝦去頭及殼、留尾；以牙籤挑出腸泥，洗淨，剪斷腹部白筋（圖1）。以刀劃開背部（圖2），再以刀背輕拍一下，入1料醃數分鐘備用。

❷紫菜皮每張切成5×10公分長方狀3片，共6片；肥豬肉切成4×9公分薄長方狀6片備用。

❸將蛋打散。油鍋燒熱抹油，倒入⅙蛋液，煎成4×9公分長方狀蛋皮，共煎6張備用。

❹每1片紫菜皮上置1份肥肉片、火腿片、萵苣、蛋皮、紅蘿蔔片，包捲成長條狀，接口處沾少許醃蝦汁黏牢備用。

❺每尾明蝦腹部朝上攤平，各包入1份紫菜捲（圖3），捲成圓筒狀，再沾裹2料，入5分熱（約100℃，200℉）油鍋，炸至金黃色，撈起瀝油，切對半即可。

■食時可沾蕃茄醬。

INGREDIENTS:

6	large prawns or shrimp
60 g. (2 oz.)	fatty pork
2	laver seaweed sheets ("nori")
2	eggs
6 (4×9 cm.) each: slices each:	leaf lettuce leaves, carrot, ham slices
4 c.	oil

①
1	egg white
3 T.	cornstarch
1 t. each:	wine, sugar, sesame oil
½ t. each:	salt, pepper

②
| 1 c. | cornstarch |
| ⅓ c. | flour |

❶ Remove head and shell of prawns, retaining the tails. Use a toothpick to remove the digestive tract, then rinse clean. Cut the underside tendons (illus. 1). Cut open but not through the backs (illus. 2), then use the side of the knife to lightly pound the prawns flat. Coat with ① and marinate for several minutes.

❷ Cut the seaweed sheets each into 3, 5×10 cm. rectangles. Slice the pork into 6 thin 4×9 cm. rectangles.

❸ Beat the eggs. Heat the wok and grease with oil. Pour in ⅙ of the beaten eggs and form into a 4×9 cm. rectangle. This is the egg skin. Do this 6 times.

❹ Place on one seaweed sheet a pork slice, ham slice, lettuce leaf, egg skin then carrot slice. Roll this into a long narrow cylinder and seal using the shrimp marinade. This is the seaweed roll.

❺ Spread each prawn out flat, then place a seaweed roll on each (illus. 3), and roll into a cylinder. Coat these with ② . Deep-fry in 100° C (200° F) oil for 5 minutes, until golden brown. Remove, drain, then cut in half to serve.

■ Ketchup may be used as a dip.

6人份　Serves 6

蜂巢蝦窩

Honeycomb Shrimp

材料：

蘆蝦或草蝦	····················	240公克
蛋	······················	4個
油	······················	6杯

①	葱段	····················	6段
	薑片	····················	3片
	蒜片	····················	$\frac{1}{2}$大匙

②	熟紅蘿蔔片、香菇片、豌豆莢		
	····················	各20公克	

③	酒、太白粉	········	各1小匙
	鹽	········	$\frac{1}{4}$小匙
	味精	········	$\frac{1}{8}$小匙
	胡椒粉	········	少許

④	高湯	········	$\frac{3}{4}$杯
	酒	········	1小匙
	鹽	········	$\frac{1}{4}$小匙
	味精、胡椒粉	········	各少許

⑤	太白粉、水	········	各1小匙
麻油	····················		1小匙
酒	····················		少許

❶蘆蝦去頭、去殼、留尾，將蝦身反折至筋斷（圖1），洗淨瀝乾水分，入③料拌勻；蛋打散；均備用。

❷將油燒至6分熱（120℃，240℉），入蝦炸至6分熟，取一漏勺將蛋液由漏勺上倒入油鍋（圖2），一絲絲凝固在蝦仁上呈餅狀；待蛋成金黃色，以漏勺將蝦餅整片撈起，上再放一漏勺（圖3），將油壓擠出來，炸油倒出備用。

❸蝦餅重新放回鍋中，開大火，沿鍋邊灑上少許酒，關火，加蓋燜一下，取出置盤排好備用。

❹鍋燒熱，入油2大匙，先入①料爆香，後入④料煮開，拌入②料，再以⑤料勾芡，灑上麻油，淋在蝦餅上即可。

6人份　Serves 6

INGREDIENTS:

240 g. (8½ oz.)		medium-sized prawns or shrimp
4		eggs
6 c.		oil
①	6 sections	green onion
	3 slices	ginger
	½ T.	sliced garlic
②	20 g. (⅔ oz.) each:	cooked carrot slices, soaked black mushroom slices, snow peas
③	1 t. each:	wine, cornstarch
	¼ t.	salt
	Dash	pepper
④	¾ c.	chicken broth
	1 t.	wine
	¼ t.	salt
	Dash	pepper
⑤	1 t. each:	cornstarch, water
1 t.		sesame oil
Dash		wine

❶ Remove head and shell, retaining tail, of shrimp. Fold body of the shrimp over until tendons break (illus. 1), then rinse and drain. Coat the shrimp with ③ Beat the eggs.

❷ Heat the oil to 120° C (240° F). Add shrimp and fry until half-cooked. Pick up a strainer and pour the beaten eggs through it and into the wok (illus. 2), creating "threads" on top of the shrimp in a cake-like shape. When the eggs turn golden brown, use the strainer to remove the whole shrimp-egg mixture from the wok at once. Place another strainer on top (illus. 3), and squeeze out the oil. Pour the oil out of the wok.

❸ Place the shrimp and egg "cake," back into the wok. Over a high flame sprinkle on wine along the sides of the wok. Turn off the burner, cover, and let sit briefly, before removing to the serving platter.

❹ Heat the wok and add 2 tablespoons of oil. Fry ① until fragrant, then add ④ and bring to a boil. Stir in ② , then ⑤ to thicken. Sprinkle on the sesame oil. Pour this sauce on the shrimp and serve.

❶

❷

❸

生炒蝦鬆

Lettuce Rolled Shrimp

材料：

明蝦或大草蝦········
·········· 240公克
油條·········· 2 條
西生菜·········· 6 片
葱末·········· 1 大匙
薑末·········· 1 小匙
油·········· 2 杯

① 竹筍（淨重）······
·········· 80公克
洋葱······60公克
西芹（淨重）······
·········· 60公克
荸薺······40公克
香菇（泡軟去蒂）······
·········· 4 朵

② 蛋白········ ¼ 個
酒········ ½ 大匙
太白粉··· 1 小匙
鹽········ ⅛ 小匙

③ 高湯········ ⅓ 杯
麻油········ 1 小匙
鹽········ ½ 小匙
味精····· ¼ 小匙
糖、胡椒粉······
·········· 各少許

④ 太白粉、水······
·········· 各 1 大匙

❶蝦去殼、去腸泥，洗淨、瀝乾水分，切小丁（圖1），入②料拌勻備用。

❷①料先切小丁（圖2），再入開水中氽燙，撈起瀝乾水分；油條亦切小丁；均備用。

❸鍋燒熱，入油2杯，將蝦丁過油，撈起瀝油備用；再入油條炸酥，撈起瀝油，置盤墊底。

❹鍋內留油3大匙，先入葱末、薑末爆香，續入①料拌炒數分鐘，再入③料拌勻，以④料勾芡，先取出½置油條上；另剩½，再入蝦丁拌勻，盛起置前項材料上。

❺將所有材料拌勻，以西生菜包食（圖3）即可。

6人份　Serves 6

INGREDIENTS

	240 g. (8½ oz.)	large prawns or shrimp
	2	fried cruller ("you tiao")
	6 leaves	lettuce
	1 T.	minced green onion
	1 t.	minced ginger
	2 c.	oil
①	80 g. (2¾ oz.)	canned bamboo shoots
	60 g. (2 oz.)	onion
	60 g. (2 oz.)	celery net weight
	40 g. (1⅓ oz.)	water chestnuts
	4	soaked, dried black mushrooms with the stems removed
②	¼	egg white
	½ T.	wine
	1 t.	cornstarch
	⅛ t.	salt
③	⅓ c.	chicken broth
	1 t.	sesame oil
	½ t.	salt
	Dash each:	sugar, pepper
④	1 T. each:	cornstarch, water

❶ Remove the shells, devein, rinse clean and drain the shrimp. Cut into small pieces (illus. 1), and coat with ② .

❷ Cut the ingredients from ① into small pieces (illus. 2). Par boil these briefly and drain. Cut the fried cruller into small pieces.

❸ Heat the wok and add 2 cups of oil. Pass the shrimp through the oil, remove and drain. Fry the fried cruller until flaky, remove and drain. Place the fried cruller on the serving platter.

❹ Retain 3 tablespoons of oil in the wok. First, add the green onion and ginger - fry until fragrant. Add ① and stir-fry several minutes. Stir in ③ , then ④ to thicken. Remove half the mixture and place on the fried cruller. Mix the other half of the mixture with the shrimp, remove, and place on top of the first half.

❺ Mix both mixtures together, and use lettuce leaves to roll them in (illus. 3).

醬肉魚丁　Meat Sauce Fish

材料：

兔魚肉	…………………	150公克
絞五花肉	…………………	80公克
熟花生(圖1)	………………	40公克
油	………………………	3 大匙
香菇丁、黑豆瓣醬	…………	各2 大匙
蒜末、蔥末、辣椒片	………	各1 大匙

①
醬油	……………………	2 大匙
酒、太白粉	……………	各1 大匙
味精、胡椒粉	…………	各 1/8 小匙

②
高湯	……………………	1 1/2 杯
酒、花生粉	……………	各1 大匙
醬油	……………………	1/2 大匙
糖	………………………	1 小匙
辣油、胡椒粉、八角粉、花椒粉		
	………………………	各少許

③ 太白粉、水	…………	各1 小匙
麻油	……………………	少許

❶兔魚肉洗淨、切小丁(圖2)，入①料醃數分
鐘備用。

❷鍋燒熱，入油3大匙，先入魚肉拌炒數下，
撈起；再入絞肉炒熟，續入黑豆瓣醬(圖3)
、蒜末、辣椒片、香菇丁炒香，再入②料及
花生，以小火燜煮4～5分鐘，最後以③料勾
芡，入兔魚肉拌勻，起鍋前灑上蔥末、麻油
即可。

INGREDIENTS:

150 g. (1/3 lb.)	fish fillet
80 g. (2¾ oz.)	ground fatty pork
40 g. (1 1/3 oz.)	cooked peanuts (illus. 1)
3 T.	oil
2 T. each:	soaked black mushroom pieces, soy bean paste
1 T. each:	minced garlic, minced green onion, sliced red chili pepper

①
2 T.	soy sauce
1 T. each:	wine, cornstarch
1/8 t.	pepper

②
1½ c.	chicken broth
1 T. each:	wine, peanut powder
½ T.	soy sauce
1 t.	sugar
Dash each:	chili oil, pepper, szechuan pepper, ground star anise

③ 1 t. each:	cornstarch, water
Dash	sesame oil

❶ Rinse the fish clean and cut into small pieces (illus. 2). Marinate in ① for several minutes.

❷ Heat the wok and add 3 table-spoons of oil. Stir-fry the fish briefly, then remove. Fry the ground pork until cooked, then add the soy bean paste (illus. 3), garlic, red chili pepper, and mushrooms. Fry until fragrant, then add ② and the peanuts. Cover and simmer this for 4-5 minutes. Stir in ③, to thicken, before stirring in fish. Lastly, sprinkle on minced green onion and sesame oil, before removing to dish and serving.

6人份　Serves 6

❶　❷　❸

6人份　Serves 6

銀魚花生

Fish Peanuts

材料：

銀魚 ………………………	100公克
蒜頭花生 …………………	60公克
油 …………………………	4杯
紅辣椒片、葱末…………	各1大匙
蒜末………………………	½大匙

①
- 酒 ……………………… ½大匙
- 鹽、糖 ………………… 各¼小匙
- 胡椒粉 ………………… 少許

❶ 銀魚洗淨，瀝乾水分（圖1）備用（若太鹹，則略泡水，圖2）。

❷ 將油燒至6分熱（約120°C，240°F），入銀魚，炸至金黃色（圖3），撈起瀝油備用。

❸ 鍋內留油2大匙，入辣椒片、葱末、蒜末爆香，再入銀魚、花生及①料拌勻即可。

INGREDIENTS:

100 g. (3½ oz.)	small steamed fish ("bu lah he")
60 g. (2 oz.)	garlic flavored peanuts
4 c.	oil
1 T. each:	sliced red chili pepper, minced green onion
½ T.	minced garlic

①
- ½ T. — wine
- ¼ t. each: — salt, sugar
- Dash — pepper

❶ Rinse the fish clean, then drain (illus. 1). If the fish are too salty, soak in water (illus. 2), and then drain.

❷ Heat the oil to 120° C (240° F), add fish and fry until golden brown (illus. 3). Remove from oil and drain.

❸ Retain 2 tablespoons of oil in wok. Add red chili pepper, green onion, garlic, and fry until fragrant; add the fish, peanuts, and ① , stir-frying until evenly mixed.

6人份　Serves 6

蠔油九孔

Oyster Sauce Abalone

材料：

大九孔	12個
西生菜	180公克
葱段	6段
薑片	4片
油	3大匙
鹽、味精	各少許
① 高湯	½杯
蠔油、醬油	各1小匙
味精	⅛小匙
② 太白粉、水	各1小匙
麻油	1小匙

❶九孔洗淨瀝乾；西生菜洗淨剁大塊(圖1)備用。

❷水燒開，入葱段、薑片及九孔，以大火煮至80℃(160°F)，關火，加蓋燜5分鐘，取出九孔，漂涼(圖2)、洗淨，去殼、去嘴(圖3)、去腸泥備用。

❸鍋燒熱，入油3大匙，再入西生菜及少許鹽、味精，大火快炒數下，盛起置盤中備用。

❹①料煮開，以②料勾芡，再入九孔拌勻，起鍋前灑上麻油，盛盤，九孔殼圍盤排齊，湯汁淋在上面即可。

INGREDIENTS:

12	abalone (slightly larger than a walnut)
180 g. (6⅓ oz.)	lettuce
6 sections	green onion
4 slices	ginger
3 T.	oil
Dash	salt
① ½ c.	chicken broth
1 t. each:	oyster sauce, soy sauce
② 1 t. each:	cornstarch, water
1 t.	sesame oil

❶ Wash the abalone and drain. Wash the lettuce and cut into large pieces (illus. 1).

❷ Bring enough water to cover the abalone to a boil. Add green onion, ginger and abalone. Cook over a high flame until the water reaches a temperature of 80° C (160° F). Turn off the burner. Cover the pan and let sit for 5 minutes. Remove abalone and cool (illus. 2); rinse, remove shell and organs (illus. 3).

❸ Heat the wok and add 3 tablespoons oil. Add lettuce and a dash of salt. Stir-fry briefly, over a high flame, then place on serving platter.

❹ Bring ① to a boil and mix in ② to thicken. Fold in abalone. Just before removing from pan sprinkle on sesame oil. Place abalone on platter. Place abalone shells around edge of platter. Pour sauce on top of the abalone.

蒜泥九孔　Garlic Puree Abalone

材料：

九孔‥‥‥‥‥‥‥‥‥‥‥‥12個	
高麗菜絲‥‥‥‥‥‥‥‥‥80公克	
葱段‥‥‥‥‥‥‥‥‥‥‥‥6段	
麻油‥‥‥‥‥‥‥‥‥‥‥2大匙	
蒜片、辣椒片‥‥‥‥‥各1大匙	

① 醬油‥‥‥‥‥‥‥‥1½大匙
　 蒜泥‥‥‥‥‥‥‥‥‥½大匙
　 酒、糖‥‥‥‥‥‥‥各1小匙
　 味精‥‥‥‥‥‥‥‥‥⅛小匙

❶九孔洗淨，燙熟(作法見蠔油九孔，第37頁)
，漂涼去嘴（圖1），翻面置殼上（圖2）備
用。

❷高麗菜絲排盤墊底；上置九孔，淋上①料，
待蒸籠水開，入蒸籠，大火蒸4分鐘，取出
備用。

❸鍋燒熱，入麻油，再入葱段、蒜片、辣椒片
爆香，淋在九孔即可。

■九孔可不去腸泥。

6人份　Serves 6

INGREDIENTS:

12	abalone (slightly larger than a walnut)
80 g. (2¾ oz.)	shredded cabbage
6 sections	green onion
2 T.	sesame oil
1 T. each:	sliced-garlic, red chili pepper

① 1½ T. soy sauce
　 ½ T. pureed garlic
　 1 t. each: wine, sugar

❶ Clean the abalone, and precook (see "OYSTER SAUCE ABALONE" page 37). Cool, and remove organs (illus. 1). Place abalone upside down on shells (illus. 2).

❷ Place cabbage on dish as a cushion for abalone. After placing abalone on cabbage, sprinkle on ① . When the water begins to steam, add steamer basket and dish with cabbage and abalone. Steam over a high flame for 4 minutes, then remove.

❸ Heat the wok and add sesame oil, then add green onion, garlic, and red chili pepper. Stir-fry until it becomes fragrant, then sprinkle over the abalone.

39

五味九孔

材料：

九孔⋯⋯⋯⋯⋯⋯⋯⋯⋯⋯12個
高麗菜絲⋯⋯⋯⋯⋯⋯⋯⋯80公克

① {
淡色醬油 ⋯⋯⋯⋯⋯⋯⋯2大匙
葱末、薑末、辣椒末、香菜末、
糖、蕃茄醬 ⋯⋯⋯⋯各½大匙
黑醋、白醋 ⋯⋯⋯⋯各1小匙
}

❶將處理好的九孔(作法見蠔油九孔，第37頁)，排在
高麗菜絲上，淋上①料即可。

■九孔可不去腸泥。

沙拉九孔

材料：

九孔 ⋯⋯⋯⋯⋯⋯⋯⋯⋯⋯12個
高麗菜 ⋯⋯⋯⋯⋯⋯⋯⋯⋯80公克
沙拉醬⋯⋯⋯⋯⋯⋯⋯⋯⋯2大匙

❶九孔洗淨，燙熟(作法見蠔油九孔，第37頁)
，去殼、去嘴、去腸泥(圖1)，切薄片 (圖
2)備用。

❷高麗菜洗淨，切細絲，排盤墊底；上置九孔
片，再淋上沙拉醬即可。

6人份　Serves 6

Five Spice Abalone

INGREDIENTS:

| 12 | abalone (slightly larger than a walnut) |
| 80 g. (2¾ oz.) | cabbage |

① {
2 T.	light soy sauce
½ T. each:	minced-green onion, ginger, red chili pepper, coriander, sugar, ketchup
1 t. each:	dark vinegar, white vinegar
}

❶ Place precooked and cleaned abalone, (done according to instructions for "OYSTER SAUCE ABALONE" page 37) on shredded cabbage. Sprinkle ① on top.

■ It is not necessary to remove intestinal tract of abalone.

Abalone Salad

INGREDIENTS:

12	abalone (slightly larger than a walnut)
80 g. (2¾ oz.)	cabbage
2 T.	mayonnaise or salad dressing

❶ Wash the abalone and precook (see "OYSTER SAUCE ABALONE" page 37). Remove the shell and organs (illus. 1), and cut into thin slices (illus. 2).

❷ Clean the cabbage and shred. Place cabbage on plate, as a cushion, then arrange abalone slices on top. Top with mayonnaise.

6 人份　Serves 6

蒜仁田腿

Garlic Frog Legs

材料：

田鷄腿 …………………………200公克	
蒜仁…………………………………30公克	
九層塔(圖1) ……………………15公克	
薑片 …………………………………3片	
油 ……………………………………4杯	
醬油膏 ………………………………1大匙	

①	高湯 ………………………4大匙
	蠔油、酒 …………………各1大匙
	醬油 ………………………1小匙
	糖…………………………½小匙
	味精………………………¼小匙
②	太白粉、水 …………………各1小匙
麻油 …………………………………1小匙

❶田鷄腿洗淨，入１大匙醬油膏拌醃(圖２)；蒜仁略拍(圖３)備用。

❷油燒至７分熱（140℃，280℉），入田鷄腿炸至金黃色，撈起瀝油備用。

❸鍋內留油２大匙，入蒜仁及薑片爆香，續入①料煮開，以②料勾芡，再倒入田鷄腿拌勻，起鍋前灑上麻油及九層塔即可。

INGREDIENTS:

200 g. (7 oz.)	frog legs
30 g. (1 oz.)	garlic
15 g. (½ oz.)	basil (illus. 1)
3 slices	ginger
4 c.	oil
1 T.	thick soy sauce

	4 T.	chicken broth
	1 T. each:	oyster sauce, wine
①	1 t.	soy sauce
	½ t.	sugar
②	1 t. each:	cornstarch, water
1 t.		sesame oil

❶ Rinse the frog legs clean and cover thoroughly with thick soy sauce, to marinate (illus. 2). Crush the garlic (illus. 3).

❷ Heat oil to 140° C (280° F). Fry the frog legs until golden brown, then remove and drain.

❸ Retain 2 tablespoons of oil in the wok. Add the garlic and ginger. Fry until fragrant. Add ① to the wok, and wait until it comes to a boil, before stirring in ② to thicken. Stir fry in the frog legs gently. Sprinkle on sesame oil and basil right before removing from wok.

芙蓉蟹

Smiling Crab

材料：

螃蟹	………………………	400公克
洋葱絲	………………………	80公克
豌豆莢	………………………	10公克
蛋白	………………………	3個
葱段	………………………	6段
麵粉	………………………	$\frac{1}{2}$ 杯
油	………………………	4杯

①
鹽	………………………	1小匙
糖	………………………	$\frac{1}{2}$ 小匙
味精	………………………	$\frac{1}{4}$ 小匙
胡椒粉	………………………	少許

❶螃蟹去腸泥，洗淨切3×3公分塊狀，沾麵粉備用。

❷將油燒至8分熱（160°C，320°F），入蟹塊炸約3分鐘，撈起（圖1）瀝油；蛋白打發；均備用。

❸另起油鍋燒熱，入油3大匙，續入葱段及洋葱絲爆香（圖2），再入①料、蟹塊及蛋白（圖3）拌炒，待蛋白呈8分熟即可。

INGREDIENTS:

400 g. (14 oz.)	crab
80 g. (2¾ oz.)	julienned onion
10 g. (⅓ oz.)	snow peas
3	egg whites
6 sections	green onions
½ c.	flour
4 c.	oil

①
1 t.	salt
½ t.	sugar
Dash	pepper

❶ Remove gills and organs from the cro
Rinse crab clean and cut into 3×3 c
pieces. Coat crab with flour.

❷ Heat oil to 160° C (320° F). Add the cro
to the oil and deep-fry for about
minutes. Remove crab and drain (illus.
Beat the egg whites.

❸ Heat 3 tablespoons of oil in the wok, th
add onion and green onion. Cook un
they emit fragrance (illus. 2). Add ① to t
wok, mix in thoroughly, then add cro
and egg white (illus. 3),stir-frying until e
white is just cooked.

6 人份　Serves 6

炒豆乳蟹

Beancurd Crab

材料：

螃蟹	400公克
洋蔥絲	120公克
蔥段	80公克
蒜片	1大匙
油	4杯

① { 蛋 …………1個
　　麵粉 ………4大匙

② {
米釀豆腐乳(圖1) ………1塊
高湯 ………1杯
酒 ………1大匙
糖 ………1小匙
鹽 ………½小匙
味精 ………¼小匙

❶螃蟹去腸泥(圖2)洗淨，切3×3公分塊狀(圖3)，入①料拌勻備用。

❷將油燒至8分熱(160℃，320°F)，入蟹塊，炸3分鐘，撈起瀝油備用。

❸另起油鍋燒熱，入油3大匙，續入蔥段、洋蔥絲、蒜片爆香，隨入②料及蟹塊拌炒至湯汁快乾時即可。

INGREDIENTS:

400 g. (14 oz.)	crab
120 g. (¼ lb.)	julienned onion
80 g. (2¾ oz.)	sections of green onion
1 T.	sliced garlic
4 c.	oil

① { 1 — egg
　　4 T. — flour

② {
1 pc. — preserved bean curd cheese (illus. 1)
1 c. — chicken broth
1 T. — wine
1 t. — sugar
½ t. — salt

❶ Remove gills and organs from crab (illus. 2), then rinse clean. Cut the crab into 3×3 cm. pieces (illus. 3), then coat with ①.

❷ Heat oil to 160° C (320° F). Place pieces of crab into wok and deep-fry for 3 minutes. Remove and drain.

❸ Reheat the wok and add 3 tablespoons of oil. Fry the onion, green onion and garlic. Cook until they emit fragrance. Add ② and crab to wok, stir-frying until sauce is almost evaporated.

砂鍋粉絲蟹

材料：

青蟹	400公克
大白菜	80公克
里肌肉	30公克
香菇	10公克
冬粉	1 把
葱段	6 段
蝦米	1 大匙
油	3 大匙
① 高湯	3 杯
醬油	1½ 大匙
鹽、味精、胡椒粉	各¼ 小匙
香菜末	1 大匙

❶青蟹去腸泥，洗淨切塊；大白菜、里肌肉均洗淨切絲；香菇泡軟切絲；蝦米泡水，瀝乾水分；粉絲泡軟；均備用。

❷鍋燒熱，入油3大匙，隨入葱段爆香，續入蝦米拌炒（圖1），再入大白菜、香菇絲、里肌肉拌勻，最後入粉絲及①料煮開備用。

❸香菜末置砂鍋內（圖2），再入❷項材料，上置蟹塊排好（圖3），入蒸籠，大火蒸5分鐘，取出砂鍋，蓋上砂鍋蓋；再將砂鍋置爐火上，以小火燜煮至香菜的香味出來即可。

■若買不到青蟹，可以紅蟳或蚶代替。

Crab with Bean Thread Casserole

INGREDIENTS:

400 g. (14 oz.)	blue crab
80 g. (2¾ oz.)	nappa cabbage
30 g. (1 oz.)	pork tenderloin
10 g. (⅓ oz.)	dried black mushrooms
1 bunch (1⅓ oz.)	bean threads
6 sections	green onion
1 T.	small dried shrimp
3 T.	oil
① 3 c.	chicken broth
1½ T.	soy sauce
¼ t. each:	salt, pepper
1 T.	minced coriander

❶ Remove the gills and organs from the crab. Rinse clean and cut into pieces. Rinse the cabbage and pork clean, then julienne. Soak the black mushroom until soft, remove stems and julienne. Soak the shrimp until soft, then drain. Separately soak the bean threads until soft.

❷ Heat the wok and add 3 tablespoons of oil. Fry the onion until fragrant, then stir-fry in the shrimp (illus. 1). Stir in the cabbage, mushrooms, and pork. Lastly, add the bean threads and ① . Bring to a boil.

❸ Place the coriander into the bottom of a casserole (illus. 2). Pour in the mixture from step ❷ , then place the crab pieces on top (illus. 3). Steam for 5 minutes over a high flame. Remove the dish from the steamer and cover. Place on burner and simmer until coriander fragrance is emitted.

■ If blue crab is unavailable then Dungeness crab may be substituted.

6人份　Serves 6

蟹肉黃瓜　Cucumber Crab Rolls

材料：

蟹肉 ………160公克
大黃瓜…………1 條
熟蛋黃…………2 個
薑汁…………1 大匙

① ┌ 荸薺絲…40公克
　　香菇絲、熟筍絲
　　……各20公克
　　葱絲…………10公克
　　└
雞油或麻油…½ 大匙

② ┌ 太白粉、麻油、
　　酒……各 1 小匙
　　鹽………½ 小匙
　　味精……¼ 小匙
　　└
③ ┌ 高湯………½ 杯
　　糖………½ 小匙
　　鹽………¼ 小匙
　　味精、胡椒粉…
　　……各少許
　　└
④ ┌ 水………1 大匙
　　太白粉…2 小匙
　　└

❶蟹肉入薑汁拌勻，再入蒸籠，大火蒸3分鐘，取出備用。

❷①料與②料先拌勻，再入蟹肉拌勻爲餡，分成12等份備用。

❸熟蛋黃入烤箱，以150℃(300°F)烤酥，待涼壓成粉末狀備用。

❹黃瓜去皮，切4公分長段(圖1)，順著圓柱狀，再切4×8公分薄片(圖2)12片，入開水中汆燙一下，撈起漂涼，瀝乾水分；每片黃瓜各放入 1 份餡，包捲成長條狀(圖3)；入蒸籠，大火蒸4分鐘，取出排盤，蒸汁留著備用。

❺③料與蒸汁煮開，以④料勾芡，起鍋前灑上雞油(或麻油)即可淋在黃瓜上，灑上蛋黃粉即可。

■周圍可以燙熟的靑江菜裝飾。

Cucumber Crab Rolls

INGREDIENTS:

160 g (5½ oz.)	crab meat
1	large cucumber
2	cooked egg yolks
1 T.	ginger juice
① 40 g. (1⅓ oz.)	julienned water chestnuts
20 g. (⅔ oz.) each:	julienned-soaked black mushrooms, canned bamboo shoots
10 g. (⅓ oz.)	shredded green onion
② 1 t. each:	cornstarch, sesame oil, wine
½ t.	salt
③ ½ c.	chicken broth
½ t.	sugar
¼ t.	salt
Dash	pepper
④ 1. T.	water
2 t.	cornstarch
½ T.	chicken fat or sesame oil

❶ Mix crab meat and ginger juice, then steam over a high flame for 3 minutes. Remove for later use.

❷ Mix ① and ② , then crab, evenly. This is the filling. Divide into 12.

❸ Place the cooked egg yolk in a 150° C (300° F) oven and bake until crispy. Cool and press into flakes.

❹ Peel the cucumber and cut into 4 cm. long sections (illus. 1). Cut again, following around the sections, to make 12, 4×8 cm. thin slices (illus. 2). Blanch, then drain and cool. Place 1 portion of filling in each cucumber slice and roll into a cylinder (illus. 3). Steam over a high flame for 4 minutes. Remove to platter. Retain juice for use in step ❺ .

❺ Bring ③ and retained juice to a boil. Thicken with ④ . Right before removing from pan, add chicken fat. Pour this on the cucumber rolls. Sprinkle egg yolk flakes on the very top.

■ Boiled "ching kang tsai", bok choy or other similar leafy green vegetable may be used to surround the cucumber rolls as an edible garnish.

6 人份　Serves 6

金茸肚絲：作法見第50頁
桂筍肉絲：作法見第51頁
蔭豉肉丁：作法見第52頁
Golden Mushroom with Pork Maw (p.50)
Bamboo and Pork Julienne (p.51)
Pork with Black Beans (p.52)

金茸肚絲

材料：
猪肚 ···················· 150公克(約½個)
竹筍(淨重) ·····················60公克
罐頭金針菇·····················60公克
芥菜心 ·····························1片
油 ·································3大匙
① ┌ 葱段 ·····························6段
　 └ 紅辣椒片、蒜片 ········各1小匙
　 ┌ 高湯 ·····························3大匙
② │ 酒 ·································1大匙
　 │ 鹽 ·······························½小匙
　 └ 味精 ·····························¼小匙
③　太白粉、水 ···············各2小匙
麻油 ·······························1小匙

❶猪肚洗淨、煮爛，切 0.5×5公分條狀備用。
❷竹筍、芥菜心分別燙熟，切與金針菇同粗細之絲狀備用。
❸鍋燒熱，入油3大匙，再入①料爆香，隨入所有材料拌炒數下，續入②料煮開，以③料勾芡，起鍋前淋上麻油即可。

■猪肚處理方法：
材料：
猪肚 ································1個
① ┌ 葱 ·································2支
　 │ 薑 ·································4片
　 └ 酒 ·································1大匙

❶猪肚以剪刀將外皮的油剪掉(圖1)；再將猪肚反面(圖2)，洗淨，以菜刀刮掉黏稠物(圖3)，再洗淨。
❷水燒開，入少許冷水令其呈7分熱(70°C，140°F)，入猪肚燙一下，撈起、洗淨；再與①料同入鍋中，以大火煮開，再改小火煮2小時至爛，取出泡冷水，洗淨即可備用。

Golden Mushroom with Pork Maw

INGREDIENTS:

150 g. (⅓ lb.)- about ½ of 1		pork maw
60 g. (2 oz.)- cooked weight		raw bamboo shoots
60 g. (2 oz.)		canned golden mushrooms
1		mustard stem
3 T.		oil
①	6 sections	green-onion
	1 t. each:	sliced red chili pepper, garlic
②	3 T.	chicken broth
	1 T.	wine
	½ t.	salt
③	2 t. each:	cornstarch, water
1 t.		sesame oil

❶ Rinse the pork maw and boil until soft. Cut into 0.5×5 cm. strips.
❷ Boil the bamboo shoots to cook them, then the mustard stem. Cut the bamboo and mustard stem into golden mushroom-sized shreds.
❸ Heat the wok and add 3 tablespoons oil. Add ① to the wok and fry until fragrant. Then add pork maw, bamboo, golden mushrooms and mustard stem. Stir fry briefly, then add ②. When this comes to a boil, stir in ③ to thicken. Sprinkle on sesame oil right before removal from wok.

■ How to clean the pork maw:
INGREDIENTS:

1		pork maw
①	2 stems	green onion
	4 slices	ginger
	1 T.	wine

❶ Use a scissors to cut fat from outside of pork maw (illus. 1). Turn inside out (illus. 2), rinse, and scrape clean (illus. 3). Rinse again.
❷ Boil water. Add a small amount of cold water to bring temperature to 70° C (140° F). Blanch the maw, then rinse. Place maw and ① in a wok and bring to a boil over a high flame. Simmer for 2 hours, until soft. Remove and soak in cold water, then rinse clean.

桂筍肉絲

Bamboo and Pork Julienne

材料：

桂竹筍	……………………	160公克
五花肉	……………………	60公克
油	……………………	1 杯
粗味噌	……………………	1 大匙

① 紅辣椒片、葱段……各 1 大匙
　　蒜片、薑片………各 1 小匙

② 太白粉………………… 1 小匙
　　醬油……………… $\frac{1}{2}$ 小匙
　　麻油……………… $\frac{1}{4}$ 小匙
　　味精、胡椒粉……各 $\frac{1}{8}$ 小匙

③ 高湯……………… 1$\frac{1}{2}$ 大匙
　　醬油……………… 1 大匙
　　糖……………… $\frac{1}{2}$ 小匙
　　味精……………… $\frac{1}{4}$ 小匙

④ 水……………… 1$\frac{1}{2}$ 大匙
　　太白粉………………… 1 小匙

麻油………………………… 少許

❶桂竹筍以手撕成絲狀(圖1)，再切 4～5公分長段(圖2)，入滾水中汆燙一下，取出洗淨瀝乾備用。

❷五花肉洗淨，切0.5公分寬絲狀(圖3)，以②料拌勻，醃數分鐘備用。

❸鍋燒熱，入油1杯，將肉絲過油，撈起瀝油備用。

❹鍋內留油3大匙，入①料爆香，再入粗味噌炒香，隨入桂竹筍及肉絲拌炒，續入③料拌勻，以④料勾芡，起鍋前灑上麻油即可。

INGREDIENTS:

160 g. (5½ oz.)		bamboo shoot strips or canned bamboo shoots
60 g. (2 oz.)		uncured bacon meat
1 c.		oil
1 T.		miso
①	1 T. each:	sliced red chili pepper, green onion sections
	1 t. each:	sliced garlic, sliced ginger
②	1 t.	cornstarch
	½ t.	soy sauce
	¼ t.	sesame oil
	⅛ t.	pepper
③	1½ T.	chicken broth
	1 T.	soy sauce
	½ t.	sugar
④	1½ T.	water
	1 t.	cornstarch
Dash		sesame oil

❶ Use fingers to shred bamboo (illus. 1). Cut the bamboo strips into 4-5 cm. lengths (illus. 2). Precook the bamboo by putting in boiling water and removing immediately, then drain.

❷ Rinse the bacon meat clean and cut into 0.5 cm. wide strips (illus. 3). Combine bacon meat and ② . Mix evenly, and marinate for several minutes.

❸ Heat the wok and add 1 cup of oil. When oil is hot, pass the meat through the oil, then remove and drain.

❹ Remove all but 3 tablespoons of oil from the wok and add ① . Fry until fragrance is emitted, then add miso and stir. Stir-fry the bamboo and meat before mixing ③ in evenly. Stir in ④, to thicken, then sprinkle the sesame oil on top just before removal from wok.

蔭豉肉丁

Pork with Black Beans

材料：

瘦豬肉	300公克
蒜苗、葱	各3支
紅辣椒	1支
蒜頭	2粒
黑豆豉	1大匙
油	3杯

① {
蛋白⋯⋯⋯⋯⋯⋯½個
醬油⋯⋯⋯⋯⋯⋯2小匙
太白粉⋯⋯⋯⋯⋯1小匙
麻油⋯⋯⋯⋯⋯⋯½小匙
小蘇打⋯⋯⋯⋯⋯⅛小匙

② {
醬油膏⋯⋯⋯⋯1½小匙
酒、白糖⋯⋯⋯各1小匙
味精⋯⋯⋯⋯⋯¼小匙

❶瘦肉以肉捶拍打，切1.5×2公分丁狀(圖1)，以②料醃10分鐘備用。

❷蒜苗、葱洗淨，切顆粒狀(圖2)；紅辣椒去籽(圖3)、與蒜頭均切小片；黑豆豉亦先處理好；均備用。

❸將油燒至3分熱(約60℃，120°F)，入肉丁過油，撈起瀝油備用。

❹鍋內留油2大匙，入❷項材料爆香，續入②料及肉丁拌勻即可。

■黑豆豉處理法同蔭豉鮮蚵(見第15頁)。

INGREDIENTS:

300 g. (⅔ lb.)	lean pork
3 stems each:	leeks, green onion
1	red chili pepper
2 cloves	garlic
1 T.	(fermented) black beans
3 c.	oil

① {
½	egg white
2 t.	soy sauce
1 t.	cornstarch
½ t.	sesame oil
⅛ t.	baking soda

② {
| 1½ t. | thick soy sauce |
| 1 t. each: | wine, white vinegar |

❶ Pound the meat, then slice into 1.5× 2 cm. rectangles (illus. 1). Marinate in ② for 10 minutes.

❷ Clean the leeks and green onion, then chop into small pieces (illus. 2). Remove the seeds from the red chili pepper (illus. 3). Cut red chili pepper and garlic into equally-sized slices. Prepare the black beans for use.

❸ Heat the oil to 60° C (120° F). Pass the pork through the oil to precook, then remove and drain.

❹ Retain 2 tablespoons of oil in the wok. Fry the ingredients from step ❷ until fragrant, then add ② and pork. Stir fry evenly.

■ See "Oysters with Black Bean Sauce" (page 15) for black bean preparation method.

蜜汁溜肉

材料：

小里肌肉 ‥‥‥‥300公克	
蝦餅（圖1）‥‥‥‥‥12片	②
檸檬汁‥‥‥‥‥ 1 大匙	
熟白芝麻‥‥‥‥‥ 1 小匙	
油‥‥‥‥‥‥‥‥ 3 杯	③

② 高湯或水‥‥‥‥ 3 大匙
醬油、麥芽 各2大匙
糖、酒‥‥‥各 1 大匙
胡椒粉‥‥‥‥‥少許
③ 太白粉、水‥各1小匙

① 蛋白‥‥‥‥‥‥½個
醬油‥‥‥‥ 1 ½ 大匙
酒、太白粉‥‥‥‥‥
‥‥‥‥‥‥各 1 大匙
味精、小蘇打‥‥‥‥
‥‥‥‥‥‥各 ⅛ 小匙

❶小里肌肉洗淨、去白筋，切厚0.5公分圓片（圖2），以肉捶輕拍一下（圖3），再以①料醃數分鐘。

❷鍋燒熱，入油3杯，燒3分熱（60°C，120°F），入肉片過油，撈起瀝油備用。

❸油鍋再燒至8分熱（160°C，320°F），入蝦餅炸酥，撈起瀝油，置盤備用。

❹鍋內留油3大匙，入②料煮開，倒入肉片拌勻，以③料勾芡，起鍋前灑上檸檬汁、熟白芝蔴，即可盛於蝦餅上。

Honey Glazed Pork

INGREDIENTS:

300 g. (⅔ lb.)	pork tenderloin
12	shrimp crackers (illus. 1)
1 T.	lemon juice
1 t.	cooked white sesame seeds
3 c.	oil

① ½ egg white
1½ T. soy sauce
1 T. each: wine, cornstarch
⅛ t. baking soda

② 3 T. chicken broth or water
2 T. each: soy sauce, malt sugar
1 T. each: sugar, wine
Dash pepper

③ 1 t. each: cornstarch, water

❶ Rinse off the meat and trim. Cut into round slices of 0.5 cm. thickness (illus. 2). Pound the meat lightly (illus. 3). Mix ① with meat and marinate for several minutes.

❷ Heat the wok and add 3 cups oil. When wok reaches 60° C (120° F), precook the meat by passing through the oil. Drain.

❸ Heat the wok to 160° C (320° F). Fry the shrimp crackers until flaky. Remove, drain and place on platter.

❹ Retain 3 tablespoons oil in wok and add ②. Bring to a boil, then stir-fry in the pork. Thicken with ③ . Right before removing from pan, sprinkle on lemon juice and sesame seeds, then place on top of shrimp crackers.

蒸蛋黃肉

材料：

絞五花肉	600公克
花瓜	80公克
蔭瓜	60公克
鹹蛋黃	4 個
鐵杯	4 個
玻璃紙	1 張
油	少許

①
花瓜汁	4 大匙
油葱酥	3 大匙
醬油	2 大匙
麻油	1 大匙
胡椒粉	$\frac{1}{4}$ 小匙
味精	少許

❶絞五花肉、蔭瓜、花瓜分別剁碎，與①料拌勻，用打數下，分成4等份備用。

❷鐵杯內抹油；玻璃紙剪成10公分之正方形4個，再放入鐵杯內(圖1)備用。

❸每個蛋黃等切成3小塊，放入鐵杯中，再將每份絞肉放入杯中，上面壓平(圖2)，共做4份；入蒸籠，大火蒸20分鐘，取出倒扣於盤(圖3)即可。

Sunshine Pork

INGREDIENTS:

600 g. (1⅓ lbs.)	ground fatty pork
80 g. (2⅔ oz.)	pickled cucumbers
60 g. (2 oz.)	fermented oriental pickling melon
4	salt-preserved egg yolks
4	metal cups
Dash	oil
1 sheet	cellophane

①
4 T.	pickled cucumber marinade
3 T.	fried shallot flakes
2 T.	soy sauce
1 T.	sesame oil
¼ t.	pepper

❶ Separately chop the pork, cucumbers, and melon, then mix together with ① . Scoop up a handful of the mixture and throw back into bowl several times. Divide the mixture into 4 separate portions.

❷ Grease the metal cups. Cut the cellophane into 4, 10 cm. squares and place inside cups (illus. 1).

❸ Cut each egg yolk into 3 pieces and place in cups. Afterwards, place meat mixture in cups pressing down flat (illus. 2). Place the four cups of meat mixture in a steamer basket and steam over a high flame for 20 minutes. Remove meat mixture from cups by inverting and tapping the cups over serving plate (illus. 3).

12人份　Serves 12

燕絲肉球

Shredded Pork Balls

材料：
瘦豬肉	450公克
肥肉	80公克
荸薺	60公克
燕皮	20張

①	蛋白	1個
	葱末	3大匙
	醬油、太白粉	各1大匙
	麻油	1小匙
	酒、鹽、糖、味精、胡椒粉	各 $\frac{1}{2}$ 小匙

❶瘦肉洗淨、去白筋(圖1)，與肥肉均以木槌槌打成泥漿狀備用。

❷燕皮切0.5公分寬絲狀(圖2)備用。

❸荸薺拍碎，擠去水分，與肉泥及①料拌勻成肉餡，分成24份，各沾裹燕皮絲(圖3)備用。

❹蒸籠鍋內水燒開，放入燕絲肉球，大火蒸7分鐘即可。

■燕皮可以蛋皮代之，即爲東坡繡球。

INGREDIENTS:
450 g. (1 lb.)	lean pork
80 g. (2¾ oz.)	fatty pork
60 g. (2 oz.)	water chestnuts
20 sheets	dried pork meat sheets ("yian pi")

①	1	egg white
	3 T.	minced green onion
	1 T. each:	soy sauce, cornstarch
	1 t.	sesame oil
	½ t. each:	wine, salt, sugar, pepper

❶ Rinse clean the lean pork and remove the tendons (illus. 1). Pound together, using a wooden mallot, the lean pork and fatty pork, until a mashed paste.

❷ Cut the dried pork meat sheets into 0.5 cm. wide strips (illus. 2).

❸ Crush the water chestnuts and squeeze dry. Mix the chestnuts with the meat paste and ① . This is the meat filling. Divide it into 24 portions. Coat each portion with the pork sheet strips (illus. 3).

❹ When the water in the steamer boils, place the pork balls in and steam over a high flame for 7 minutes, until done.

■ Egg sheets may be substituted for dried pork meat sheets, becoming "Shredded Egg Balls."

油條雙脆

Double Crispy Delight

材料：

腰子	……………………………	1 副
油條	……………………………	1 條
海蜇皮	…………………………	160 公克
豌豆莢	…………………………	50公克
蒜頭	……………………………	3 粒
葱	………………………………	2 支
油	………………………………	2 杯

	高湯或水	…………………	2 大匙
	黑醋	……………………	1 $\frac{1}{2}$ 小匙
①	糖、醬油	………………	各 1 小匙
	白醋、鹽	………………	各 $\frac{1}{4}$ 小匙
	胡椒粉、味精	…………	各少許
②	太白粉、水	……………	各 1 大匙
麻油	………………………	少許

❶腰子切開、去白筋（圖1），洗淨切花片（圖2），泡水10分鐘取出，入開水汆燙至 7 分熟，撈起漂涼；海蜇皮先泡水約 4 小時，取出洗淨，切 3×4公分片狀，再入70℃（140℉）熱水中汆燙一下，撈起漂涼備用。

❷蒸籠鍋內水燒開，入油條蒸軟（圖3），取出切 3 公分長段；蒜頭切片、葱切段；均備用。

❸油燒至 7 分熱（約140℃，280℉），入油條炸酥，撈起瀝油，排盤墊底備用。

❹鍋內留油 3 大匙，先入蒜片及葱段爆香，續入①料拌勻，再以②料勾芡，隨入腰片及海蜇皮拌勻，起鍋前灑上少許麻油，盛起置於油條上即可。

INGREDIENTS:

1	pork kidney
1	fried cruller ("you tiao")
160 g. (5½ oz.)	jellyfish
50 g. (1¾ oz.)	snow peas
3 cloves	garlic
2 stems	green onion
2 c.	oil

	2 T.	chicken broth or water
	1½ t.	dark vinegar
①	1 t. each:	sugar, soy sauce
	¼ t. each:	white vinegar, salt
	Dash	pepper
②	1 T. each:	cornstarch, water
Dash		sesame oil

❶ Cut the kidney open and remove tendons (illus. 1). Rinse clean and butterfly (illus. 2). Soak in water for 10 minutes, then precook in boiling water until medium rare. Remove and cool. Soak the jellyfish for approximately 4 hours. Remove, rinse clean, then cut into 3×4 cm. slices. Blanch the jellyfish in 70° C (140° F) water. Remove and cool.

❷ When the steamer water begins to boil, add fried cruller. Steam until soft (illus. 3). Remove and cut into 3 cm. lengths. Slice garlic and cut green onion into sections.

❸ Heat the oil to 140° C (280° F). Fry fried cruller until crispy, then drain and place on top of platter.

❹ Remove all but 3 tablespoons oil. Cook garlic and green onion until fragrant, then stir fry in ① . Thicken with ② . Add kidney and jellyfish. Stir-fry until ingredients are even throughout. Sprinkle on sesame oil just before removing from pan, then place mixture on top of fried cruller.

6 人份　Serves 6

西芹鷄片：作法見第60頁
雪茸鷄球：作法見第61頁
葱燒去骨鷄：作法見第62頁

Celery Chicken (p.60)
Snow Chicken Balls (p.61)
Onion Chicken Fillet (p.62)

西芹鷄片

Celery Chicken

材料：

鷄胸肉	⋯⋯⋯⋯⋯⋯240公克
西芹片	⋯⋯⋯⋯⋯⋯80公克
香菇片	⋯⋯⋯⋯⋯⋯20公克
紅蘿蔔片	⋯⋯⋯⋯⋯15公克
油	⋯⋯⋯⋯⋯⋯⋯4杯
蒜片、薑片、辣椒片	⋯⋯各1大匙

①	蛋白 ⋯⋯⋯⋯⋯⋯½個
	酒 ⋯⋯⋯⋯⋯⋯1小匙
	太白粉 ⋯⋯⋯⋯½小匙
	鹽、味精 ⋯⋯各¼小匙
	小蘇打或嫩精 ⋯⅛小匙

②	高湯 ⋯⋯⋯⋯⋯¾杯
	鹽 ⋯⋯⋯⋯⋯¼小匙
	味精 ⋯⋯⋯⋯⅛小匙
	胡椒粉 ⋯⋯⋯⋯少許

③	太白粉、水⋯⋯⋯各1小匙
麻油	⋯⋯⋯⋯⋯⋯1小匙

❶鷄胸肉洗淨，切薄片（圖1），入①料拌匀；將油燒至3分熱（60℃，120℉），入鷄片過油（圖2），撈起備用。

❷西芹片及紅蘿蔔片入開水汆燙一下（圖3）備用。

❸鍋燒熱，入油3大匙，續入蒜片、薑片、辣椒片、香菇片爆香，再入②料及鷄片、西芹片、紅蘿蔔拌匀，以③料勾芡，起鍋前灑上麻油即可。

INGREDIENTS:

240 g. (8½ oz.)	chicken breast fillets
80 g. (2¾ oz.)	sliced celery
20 g. (⅔ oz.)	sliced, soaked black mushroom
15 g. (½ oz.)	sliced carrot
4 c.	oil
1 T. each:	sliced - garlic, ginger, red chili pepper

①	½	egg white
	1 t.	wine
	½ t.	cornstarch
	¼ t.	salt
	⅛ t.	baking soda or tenderizer

②	¾ c.	chicken broth
	¼ t.	salt
	Dash	pepper

③	1 t. each:	cornstarch, water
	1 t.	sesame oil

❶ Wash chicken breast and slice into thin pieces (illus. 1), then coat thoroughly with ① . Heat oil in wok to 60° C (120° F). Precook the chicken by passing through oil (illus. 2). Drain.

❷ Parboil the celery and carrot (illus. 3).

❸ Heat 3 tablespoons of oil in the wok, then add garlic, ginger, red chili pepper and mushroom. When they begin to emit their fragrance add ② , chicken, celery and carrot. Stir fry, mixing thoroughly, then add ③ to thicken. Right before removing from heat sprinkle on sesame oil.

雪茸鷄球

Snow Chicken Balls

材料：

鷄胸肉	240公克
絞肥肉	40公克
豌豆莢	40公克
紅蘿蔔、草菇	各20公克
乾白木耳(圖1)	5公克
洋葱末	$\frac{1}{4}$杯
油	2大匙

① 紅辣椒片、蒜片、薑片 ‥各$\frac{1}{2}$大匙

②	蛋白	$\frac{1}{2}$個
	太白粉	2大匙
	酒	2小匙
	醬油	1小匙
	薑汁	$\frac{1}{2}$小匙
	鹽、胡椒粉	各$\frac{1}{4}$小匙
	味精	$\frac{1}{8}$小匙

③	高湯	1杯
	糖	$\frac{1}{2}$小匙
	鹽	$\frac{1}{4}$小匙
	味精	$\frac{1}{8}$小匙

④	太白粉	2大匙
	水	$1\frac{1}{2}$大匙

麻油、鷄油 …… 各$\frac{1}{2}$小匙

❶鷄胸肉洗淨、剁碎，拌入絞肥肉，續剁成泥狀，入洋葱末及②料拌勻，甩打數下備用。

❷豌豆莢去蒂、洗淨；紅蘿蔔洗淨，切小片(圖2)；白木耳泡軟、去蒂、洗淨；草菇切片；均入開水中汆燙，撈起漂涼備用。

❸鍋中水再煮開，將鷄泥擠成丸子狀(圖3)，入鍋汆燙，待熟撈起備用。

❹鍋燒熱，入油2大匙，續入①料爆香，隨入③料及燙好的❷項材料拌勻，煮開，以④料勾芡，最後拌入鷄球，起鍋前灑上麻油及鷄油即可。

INGREDIENTS:

240 g. (8½ oz.)	chicken breast fillet
40 g. (1⅓ oz.)	ground fatty pork
40 g. (1⅓ oz.)	snow peas
20 g. (⅔ oz.) each:	carrot, straw mushrooms
5 g. (⅙ oz.)	dried white fungus (illus. 1)
¼ c.	minced onion
2 T.	oil

①	½ T. each:	sliced - red chili pepper, garlic, ginger

②	½	egg white
	2 T.	cornstarch
	2 t.	wine
	1 t.	soy sauce
	½ t.	ginger juice
	¼ t. each:	salt, pepper

③	1 c.	chicken broth
	½ t.	sugar
	¼ t.	salt

④	2 T.	cornstarch
	1½ T.	water

½ t. each:	sesame oil, chicken fat

❶ Rinse the chicken clean, chop into small pieces, and mix with the ground pork. Continue to chop the meats until this becomes a mash. Mix the mash evenly with the minced onion and ② . Use hand to scoop out a handful of the mixture from the bowl and throw back in. Do this several times.

❷ Remove stems and strings from the snow peas, then rinse clean. Rinse the carrot clean and cut into small slices (illus. 2). Soak the white fungus, remove stems and rinse clean. Slice the straw mushrooms. Par boil these briefly in boiling water; remove and cool.

❸ Bring the water in the wok to a boil once again. Squeeze the meat mash into ball shapes (illus. 3), using hand. Place the balls in the water until cooked, then remove for later use.

❹ Heat the wok and add 2 tablespoons of oil. Fry ① until fragrant, then add ③ and the ingredients from step ❷ . Mix these thoroughly and bring to a boil. Stir in ④ to thicken. Lastly, stir in the chicken balls. Sprinkle on the sesame oil and chicken fat just before removing from the wok to a serving dish.

6 人份 Serves 6

葱燒去骨鷄

Onion Chicken Fillet

材料：

鷄腿	600公克
靑江菜（圖１）	240公克
蒜頭	40公克
葱段	25公克
油	4杯
醬油膏	1大匙
麻油	1小匙
① 高湯	2杯
醬油	1大匙
酒	½大匙
糖	½小匙
味精、胡椒粉	各少許
② 太白粉、水	各1小匙
鹽、味精、水	各少許

❶鷄腿去骨（圖２），洗淨瀝乾，入１大匙醬油膏拌醃５分鐘；靑江菜洗淨備用。

❷油燒至７分熱（140℃，280°F），入鷄腿炸至金黃色，撈起瀝油備用。

❸鍋燒熱，入油２大匙，先入葱段及蒜頭爆香，續入①料及炸好的鷄腿，以小火煮約10分鐘，取出鷄腿，切成１×５公分片狀（圖３），湯汁備用。

❹鍋燒熱，入油２大匙，入靑江菜拌炒數下，續入少許鹽、味精、水拌勻，盛起排盤墊底，鷄塊置其上備用。

❺將煮鷄腿的湯汁煮開，以②料勾芡，灑上麻油，淋在鷄塊上即可。

INGREDIENTS:

600 g. (1⅓ lb.)	chicken legs
240 g. (8½ oz.)	green cabbage ("ching kang tsai"), or other green leafy vegetable (illus. 1)
40 g. (1⅓ oz.)	garlic
25 g. (¾ oz.)	green onion sections
4 c.	oil
1 T.	thick soy sauce
1 t.	sesame oil
① 2 c.	chicken broth
1 T.	soy sauce
½ T.	wine
½ t.	sugar
Dash	pepper
② 1 t. each:	cornstarch, water
Dash each:	salt, water

❶ Remove the bones from the legs (illus. 2), rinse clean and drain. Coat with 1 tablespoon thick soy sauce and let marinate for 5 minutes. Wash the green cabbage.

❷ Heat the oil to 140° C (280° F).Deep-fry the chicken until golden brown. Remove and drain.

❸ Heat the wok and add 2 tablespoons of oil. Fry the green onion and garlic until fragrant, then add ① and the fried chicken. Over a low flame simmer this for 10 minutes. Remove the chicken legs and cut into slices of 1×5 cm. (illus. 3). Retain the sauce.

❹ Heat the wok and add 2 tablespoons of oil. Stir-fry the green cabbage briefly, then stir in a dash each of salt and water. Remove, and place on the serving platter. Place the chicken on top of the green cabbage. Bring the sauce from step ❸ to a boil. Stir in ②, to thicken, and sprinkle on the sesame oil. Pour this sauce on top of the chicken.

6 人份　Serves 6

杏仁鷄片

Almond Chicken Slices

材料：

鷄胸肉	………………………	240公克
杏仁片(圖1)	………………	120公克
油	………………………………	3 杯

①	蛋白	…………………………	1個
	麵粉	…………………………	1大匙
	酒、麻油	………………	各1小匙
	鹽	………………………	$\frac{1}{2}$小匙
	味精	………………………	$\frac{1}{4}$小匙
	胡椒粉	…………………	$\frac{1}{8}$小匙

❶鷄胸肉切3×6公分薄片(圖2)，入①料拌醃10分鐘備用。

❷將醃好的鷄胸肉沾上杏仁片(圖3)備用。

❸油燒至7分熱(140℃，280°F)，入鷄片炸至金黃色，撈起瀝油即可。

■若買不到杏仁片可以芝麻、核桃或瓜子仁代替，而爲芝麻鷄片、核桃鷄片、瓜子鷄片。

INGREDIENTS:

240 g (8½ oz.)	chicken breast fillets
120 g (4¼ oz.)	almond slices (illus. 1)
3 c.	oil

①	1	egg white
	1 T.	flour
	1 t. each:	wine, sesame oil
	½ t.	salt
	⅛ t.	pepper

❶ Cut chicken into 3×6 cm. thin slices (illus. 2). Mix with ① and marinate for 10 minutes.

❷ Coat the marinated chicken with almonds (illus. 3).

❸ Heat oil in wok to 140° C (280° F). Fry chicken until golden brown, then drain.

■ If sliced almonds are unavailable, sesame seeds, walnuts, or watermelon seeds may be used instead. If so, then the recipe becomes "Sesame Chicken Slices," "Walnut Chicken Slices," or "Watermelon Seed Chicken Slices," accordingly.

63

6人份　Serves 6

鹽酥雞塊

Flaky Chicken

材料：

半土鷄	……………………	300公克
油	……………………	4 杯

①
- 蛋 ……………………1個
- 酒 ……………………1½小匙
- 鹽、味精…………各½小匙
- 地瓜粉…………………少許

②
- 麻油……………………½大匙
- 酒 ……………………1小匙
- 黑胡椒粉………………½小匙
- 鹽……………………⅛小匙

❶鷄洗淨，剁約4×4公分大小（圖1），入①料拌勻備用。

❷油燒至8分熱（160℃，320°F），入醃好的鷄塊，炸至金黃色，撈起瀝油（圖2）備用。

❸油鍋的油倒出，再入鷄塊及②料拌勻（圖3）即可。

INGREDIENTS:

300 g. (⅔ lb.)		chicken
4 c.		oil

①
- 1 egg
- 1½ t. wine
- ½ t. salt
- Dash sweet potato powder

②
- ½ T. sesame oil
- 1 t. wine
- ½ t. pepper
- ⅛ t. salt

❶ Rinse the chicken clean and cut into 4×4 cm. pieces (illus. 1). Coat chicken with ① .

❷ Heat oil to 160° C (320° F). Fry coated chicken pieces until golden brown, then drain (illus. 2).

❸ Remove oil from wok, then add the chicken and ② . Stir-fry until well mixed (illus. 3).

6 人份　Serves 6

腰果牛鬆

材料：
絞牛肉‥‥‥‥‥‥‥‥‥240公克
炸腰果‥‥‥‥‥‥‥‥‥‥$\frac{1}{4}$杯
西生菜‥‥‥‥‥‥‥‥‥‥‥6片
油‥‥‥‥‥‥‥‥‥‥‥‥3大匙
香菜末‥‥‥‥‥‥‥‥‥‥1大匙
①　{ 蛋白‥‥‥‥‥‥‥‥‥‥‥1個
　　水‥‥‥‥‥‥‥‥‥‥‥4大匙
　　太白粉‥‥‥‥‥‥‥‥$\frac{1}{2}$大匙
　　鹽、嫩精‥‥‥‥‥各$\frac{1}{4}$小匙
　　味精‥‥‥‥‥‥‥‥$\frac{1}{8}$小匙
②　{ 白醬油、酒‥‥‥‥‥各1大匙
　　黑胡椒粉‥‥‥‥‥‥$\frac{1}{2}$小匙
　　味精‥‥‥‥‥‥‥‥$\frac{1}{4}$小匙

❶絞牛肉入①料拌匀，再入1大匙油拌匀備用。
❷西生菜剪成圓形如杯狀（圖1）；腰果切碎備用。
❸鍋燒熱，入油2大匙，再入牛肉及②料、香菜末拌
　炒（圖2），盛盤，分成6等份備用。
❹每片西生菜各置1份牛鬆，灑上腰果（圖3）即可。

Lettuce Cups with Beef and Cashews

INGREDIENTS:

240 g. (8½ oz.)		ground beef
¼ c.		fried cashews
6 leaves		lettuce
3 T.		oil
1 T.		minced coriander
①	1	egg white
	4 T.	water
	½ T.	cornstarch
	¼ t. each:	salt, tenderizer
②	1 T. each:	light soy sauce, wine
	½ t.	pepper

❶ Mix together the ground beef and ① , then mix in 1 tablespoon oil.

❷ Cut the lettuce into round pieces, to be used as cups (illus. 1). Chop the cashew nuts.

❸ Heat the wok and add 2 tablespoons oil. First add the beef, then ② and the coriander (illus. 2). Stir-fry until done. Remove to platter and divide into 6 portions.

❹ Place one portion of the beef mixture on each leaf of lettuce. Sprinkle cashew nuts on top (illus. 3), and serve.

葱爆牛肉：作法見第68頁
銀芽牛肉：作法見第69頁
韭黃牛肉：作法見第70頁

Exploding Onion Beef (p.68)
Silver Sprout Beef (p.69)
Beef and Yellow Chinese Chives (p.70)

葱爆牛肉 | # Exploding Onion Beef

材料：

牛肉	250公克
葱	120公克
油	4杯

① 辣椒片 ·············1大匙
　 蒜片 ·············½大匙
　 薑末 ·············1小匙

② 蛋白 ·············½個
　 水 ·············3大匙
　 太白粉 ·············1大匙
　 醬油 ·············½大匙
　 嫩精 ·············¼小匙
　 味精 ·············⅛小匙

③ 酒 ·············1大匙
　 醬油 ·············½大匙
　 蠔油 ·············2小匙
　 麻油 ·············1小匙

④ 太白粉、水 ·········各½小匙

❶牛肉切1×6公分條狀(圖1)，入②料拌勻，以1杯油醃泡(圖2)備用。

❷葱洗淨，切3公分長段備用。

❸鍋燒熱，入油3杯，燒至3分熱(60°C，120°F)，入牛肉過油，撈起瀝油；再將油燒至7分熱(140°C，280°F)，入葱段過油(圖3)，撈起瀝油備用。

❹鍋內留油2大匙，入①料爆香，續入牛肉、葱段及③料拌勻，最後以④料勾芡即可。

INGREDIENTS:

250 g. (8¾ oz.)	beef
120 g. (¼ lb.)	green onion
4 c.	oil

① 1 T. — sliced red chili pepper
　 ½ T. — sliced garlic
　 1 t. — minced ginger

② ½ — egg white
　 3 T. — water
　 1 T. — cornstarch
　 ½ T. — soy sauce
　 ¼ t. — tenderizer

③ 1 T. — wine
　 ½ T. — soy sauce
　 2 t. — oyster sauce
　 1 t. — sesame oil

④ ½ t. each: cornstarch, water

❶ Cut the beef into 1×6 cm. rectangles (illus. 1). Mix ② in evenly with beef, then marinate in 1 cup oil (illus. 2).

❷ Clean the onion and cut into 3 cm. long sections.

❸ Heat the wok and add 3 cups of oil. Let the oil warm to 60° C (120° F). Precook the beef by passing through oil. Remove and drain. Reheat the oil to 140° C (280° F), then precook the onion by also passing through oil (illus. 3). Remove and drain.

❹ Pour off all but 2 tablespoons of the oil and add ① . When ① gives off fragrance add beef, onion and ③ . Stir-fry thoroughly. Stir in ④, to thicken, then serve.

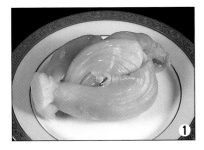

銀芽牛肉

Silver Sprout Beef

材料：

豆芽	180公克
牛肉	160公克
酸菜（圖1）	40公克
油	3杯

① { 薑末、蒜末、辣椒絲…各1小匙
　　葱段 …………………………6段

② { 蛋白 ……………………… $\frac{1}{3}$ 個
　　水 ………………………… 2大匙
　　太白粉 ………………… $\frac{1}{2}$ 大匙
　　醬油 ……………………… 1小匙
　　嫩精 ………………… $\frac{1}{4}$ 小匙
　　味精 ………………… $\frac{1}{8}$ 小匙

③ { 蠔油 ……………………… 1大匙
　　麻油 ……………………… 1小匙
　　糖 ………………… $\frac{1}{2}$ 小匙
　　味精 ………………… $\frac{1}{4}$ 小匙

④　太白粉、水 …………各1小匙

❶牛肉切粗絲，入②料拌勻，再加1大匙油拌勻；豆芽洗淨、去頭尾，即爲銀芽；酸菜切絲；均備用。

❷鍋燒熱，入油3杯，燒至3分熟(60℃,120°F)，入牛肉絲過油，撈起瀝油；再將油燒至7分熱(140℃，280°F)，入銀芽過油(圖2)，撈起瀝油備用。

❸鍋內留油3大匙，入①料爆香(圖3)，隨入牛肉、銀芽、酸菜絲及③料大火快炒，起鍋前以④料勾芡即可。

INGREDIENTS:

180 g. (6⅓ oz.)	snow mung bean sprouts
160 g. (5½ oz.)	beef
40 g. (1⅓ oz.)	pickled mustard greens (illus. 1)
3 c.	oil

① { 1 t. each: shredded red chili pepper, minced ginger, minced garlic
　　6 sections green onion

② { ⅓ egg white
　　2 T. water
　　½ T. cornstarch
　　1 t. soy sauce
　　¼ t. tenderizer

③ { 1 T. oyster sauce
　　1 t. sesame oil
　　½ t. sugar

④　1 t. each: cornstarch, water

❶ Cut the beef into strips. Mix ② with the beef, then mix in 1 tablespoon of oil. Remove both ends of the snow mung bean sprouts and wash. Cut the pickled mustard greens into fine strips.

❷ Heat the wok before adding 3 cups of oil and heating to 60° C (120° F). Pass the beef through the oil, then remove and drain. Reheat the oil to 140° C (280° F). Pass the bean sprouts through the oil (illus. 2), then remove and drain.

❸ Remove all but 3 tablespoons of oil from the wok, then add ①. Fry until fragrance is emitted (illus. 3), then add beef, bean sprouts, pickled mustard and ③. Stir-fry this over a high flame. Just before removing from the wok, stir in ④, to thicken, then serve.

韮黃牛肉

Beef and Yellow Chinese Chives

材料：

牛肉	·············	160公克
韮黃	·············	100公克
油	·············	3杯

① 葱段 ············· 6段
　蕾末、蒜末 ············· 各1小匙

② 蛋白 ············· $\frac{1}{3}$個
　水 ············· 2大匙
　太白粉 ············· $\frac{1}{2}$大匙
　醬油 ············· 1小匙
　嫩精 ············· $\frac{1}{4}$小匙
　味精 ············· $\frac{1}{8}$小匙

③ 醬油 ············· 1大匙
　蠔油 ············· $\frac{1}{2}$大匙
　糖 ············· $\frac{1}{4}$小匙
　味精、麻油 ············· 各少許

④ 太白粉、水 ············· 各1小匙

❶牛肉切絲(圖1)，入②料拌勻，再加油1大匙拌勻備用。

❷韮黃洗淨，切4公分長段(圖2)備用。

❸鍋燒熱，入油3杯，燒至3分熱(60℃,120℉)，入牛肉絲過油，撈起瀝油備用。

❹鍋內留油2大匙，入①料爆香，續入韮黃拌炒（圖3），隨入牛肉絲及③料拌勻，再以④料勾茨即可。

INGREDIENTS:

160 g. (5½ oz.)		beef
100 g. (3½ oz.)		yellow Chinese chives
3 c.		oil

① 6 sections — green onion
　1 t. each: — minced garlic, minced ginger

② 1/3 — egg white
　2 T. — water
　½ T. — cornstarch
　1 t. — soy sauce
　¼ t. — tenderizer

③ 1 T. — soy sauce
　½ T. — oyster sauce
　¼ t. — sugar
　Dash — sesame oil

④ 1 t. each: — cornstarch, water

❶ Cut the beef into strips (illus. 1). Add ② to beef and mix evenly, then marinate in 1 tablespoon of oil.

❷ Clean the chives and cut into 4 cm. long sections (illus. 2).

❸ Heat the wok and add 3 cups of oil. When the oil reaches a temperature of 60° C (120° F), pass the beef through the oil, and remove and drain.

❹ Remove all but 2 tablespoons of oil from the wok. First, stir-fry ① until it emits fragrance. Add chives and stir-fry (illus. 3), before mixing in thoroughly the beef and ③. Add ④, to thicken, then serve.

6 人份　Serves 6

干煎牛排

Sautéed Steak

6 人份　Serves 6

材料：

沙朗牛肉	……………………	300公克
洋葱末	…………………………	1 大匙
蒜末	……………………………	1 小匙
油	………………………………	3 杯

①
蛋白	…………………………… $\frac{1}{2}$ 個
醬油、太白粉	………… 各 1 大匙
水	…………………………… 1 小匙
嫩精(圖1)、糖	……各 $\frac{1}{8}$ 小匙

②
醬油膏、酒	…………各 1 大匙
蕃茄醬	…………………… $\frac{1}{2}$ 大匙
糖	…………………………… 1 小匙
黑胡椒粉、醋	……各 $\frac{1}{2}$ 小匙
味精	…………………………… 少許

❶沙朗牛肉切成6等份片狀(圖2)，入①料拌匀，再加 1大匙油醃約半小時備用。

❷鍋燒熱，入油3杯，燒至5分熱(100°C，200°F)，入 牛肉過油(圖3)，撈起瀝油備用。

❸鍋內留油2大匙，先入洋葱末及蒜末爆香，隨入② 料煮開，再入牛排燜至7～8分熟即可。

INGREDIENTS:

300 g. (²⁄₃ lb.)		beef sirloin
1 T.		minced onion
1 t.		minced garlic
3 c.		oil
①	½	egg white
	1 T. each:	soy sauce, cornstarch
	1 t.	water
	⅛ t. each:	tenderizer (illus. 1), sugar
②	1 T. each:	thick soy sauce, wine
	½ T.	ketchup
	1 t.	sugar
	½ t.	pepper, vinegar

❶ Cut the steak into 6 equal slices (illus. 2). Mix with ①, then add 1 tablespoon oil. Marinate for half an hour.

❷ Heat the wok and add 3 cups of oil. When the oil reaches 100° C (200° F), pass the beef through the oil (illus. 3). Remove beef and drain.

❸ Retain 2 tablespoons of oil in the wok. First add onion and garlic. Cook until fragrant, then add ②; when this comes to a boil, add the beef. Cover and simmer until the beef is medium rare, then remove and serve.

冬菇芥菜：作法見第74頁
韭黃炒四絲：作法見第75頁
扁魚白菜：作法見第76頁
Mushrooms and Mustard Greens (P.74)
Chives and Friends (P.75)
Fish-flavored Cabbage (P.76)

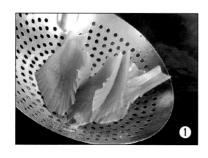

冬菇芥菜

Mushrooms and Mustard Greens

材料：

芥菜	····················	240公克
香菇	····················	40公克
油	····················	3 大匙
蒜末	····················	1 小匙

①	高湯	··········	3 大匙
	酒	··········	1 小匙
	鹽	··········	$\frac{1}{2}$ 小匙
	味精	··········	$\frac{1}{4}$ 小匙

②	高湯	··········	1 杯
	蠔油	··········	1 大匙
	辣醬	··········	$\frac{1}{2}$ 小匙
	味精	··········	$\frac{1}{4}$ 小匙
	胡椒粉	··········	$\frac{1}{8}$ 小匙

③	水	··········	1 小匙
	太白粉	··········	$\frac{1}{2}$ 小匙

麻油	····················	1 小匙

❶芥菜洗淨，入開水中氽燙至軟(圖1)，取出漂涼，切箭形狀備用。

❷鍋燒熱，入油3大匙，先入蒜末爆香，再入芥菜及①料拌勻，取出排盤(圖2)備用。

❸香菇泡軟、洗淨、去蒂、瀝乾備用。

❹②料煮開，入香菇，以小火燜煮至湯汁剩$\frac{1}{2}$時，撈起香菇，排在芥菜上(圖3)；湯汁以③料勾芡，灑上麻油，淋在香菇上即可。

INGREDIENTS:

240 g. (8½ oz.)		mustard greens
40 g. (1⅓ oz.)		dried black mushrooms
3 T.		oil
1 t.		minced garlic
①	3 T.	chicken broth
	1 t.	wine
	½ t.	salt
②	1 c.	chicken broth
	1 T.	oyster sauce
	½ t.	hot sauce
	⅛ t.	pepper
③	1 t.	water
	½ t.	cornstarch
1 t.		sesame oil

❶ Rinse the mustard greens clean, then parboil until soft (illus. 1). Remove, cool, and cut into spear-shaped pieces.

❷ Heat the wok and add 3 tablespoons of oil. Fry garlic until fragrant. Mix in mustard greens and ① . Remove to the serving platter (illus. 2).

❸ Soak the mushrooms, rinse clean, remove stems and drain.

❹ Bring ② to a boil, then add the mushrooms. Cover, and over a low flame boil down until only one-half the original amount of sauce remains. Remove the mushrooms and place on top of the mustard greens (illus. 3). Stir ③ into the sauce to thicken, spirnkle on sesame oil, then pour the sauce on top of the mushrooms.

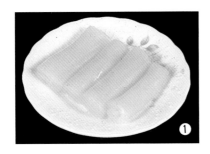

韭黃炒四絲

Chives and Friends

材料：
韭黃	……………………	100公克
里肌肉	……………………	40公克
豆干、榨菜絲	……………	各40公克
粉皮卷（圖1）	……………	1卷
油	……………………	1杯

① 葱段 …………………………6段
　 紅辣椒絲、蒜片………各1小匙
② 醬油、味精、蛋白、太白粉……
　 …………………………各少許
③ 鹽 ……………………………½小匙
　 味精 …………………………¼小匙
④ 太白粉、水 ……………各1小匙
　 麻油 …………………………少許

❶韭黃洗淨，切5公分長段；里肌肉切細絲，入②料拌勻；粉皮卷及豆干均切絲（圖2）備用。
❷鍋燒熱，入油1杯，燒至4分熱（80℃，160°F），入肉絲及豆干絲過油（圖3），撈起瀝油備用。
❸鍋內留油3大匙，先入①料爆香，再入所有材料及③料拌勻，以④料勾芡，起鍋前灑上麻油即可。

INGREDIENTS:
100 g. (3½ oz.)	yellow Chinese chives
40 g. (1⅓ oz.) each:	pork tenderloin, pressed bean curd, shredded, pickled mustard greens
1	mung bean roll (illus. 1)
1 c.	oil
Dash	sesame oil

① 6 sections　green onion
　 1 t. each:　shredded red chili pepper, sliced garlic
② Dash each:　soy sauce, egg white, cornstarch
③ ½ t.　salt
④ 1 t. each:　cornstarch, water

❶ Clean the chives and cut into 5 cm. lengths. Cut pork into fine strips and mix with ② . Cut mung bean rolls and pressed bean curd into equally sized fine strips (illus. 2).
❷ Heat the wok and add 1 cup of oil. Heat to 80° C (160° F), then pass pork and pressed bean curd through the oil to precook (illus. 3). Drain.
❸ Retain 3 tablespoons of oil in wok. Fry ① until fragrant, then add all main ingredients and ③ . Stir in ④ to thicken. Sprinkle on sesame oil just before removing from wok.

扁魚白菜

材料：

大白菜	………………	300公克
里肌肉	………………	60公克
扁魚	………………	40公克
香菇	………………	3 朵
蔥段	………………	4 段
蒜片	………………	½ 大匙
油	………………	2 杯

① 蛋白……………… ¼ 個
醬油、太白粉……… 各 1 小匙
味精……………… 少許

② 高湯……………… 2 杯
糖……………… 1 小匙
鹽……………… ¾ 小匙
味精……………… 少許

③ 酒、黑醋……………… 各 1 小匙
④ 太白粉、水 ……… 各1½ 小匙
麻油……………… 1 小匙

❶大白菜洗淨，切4公分長片狀，入開水汆燙至軟（圖1），撈起備用。

❷香菇泡軟、去蒂切片；里肌肉切片，入①料拌勻；扁魚切小片（圖2）；均備用。

❸將油2杯入鍋，燒至3分熱(60℃，120°F)，先入肉片過油，撈起瀝油備用；再將油燒至8分熱(160℃，320°F)，隨入香菇過油，撈起瀝油；再入扁魚炸酥（圖3），撈起瀝油備用。

❹鍋內留油3大匙，入蒜片及蔥段爆香，續入②料及白菜、肉片、香菇、扁魚，以大火煮開，改小火燜煮至湯汁快收乾時，入③料拌勻，以④料勾芡，起鍋前灑上麻油即可。

Fish-Flavored Cabbage

INGREDIENTS:

300 g. (⅔ lb.)	nappa cabbage
60 g. (2 oz.)	pork tenderloin
40 g. (1⅓ oz.)	dried flat fish
3	dried black mushrooms
4 sections	green onion
½ T.	sliced garlic
2 c.	oil

① ¼ egg white
1 t. each: soy sauce, cornstarch

② 2 c. chicken stock
1 t. sugar
¾ t. salt

③ 1 t. each: wine, dark vinegar
④ 1½ t. each: cornstarch, water
1 t. sesame oil

❶ Rinse the cabbage clean and cut into 4 cm. long slices. Par boil until soft (illus. 1). Remove for later use.

❷ Soak the mushrooms until soft, remove stems and slice. Slice the pork and coat with ① . Slice the fish (illus. 2).

❸ Add 2 cups of oil to the wok and heat to 60° C (120° F). Pass the pork through the oil. Remove and drain. Heat the oil to 160° C (320° F). Pass the mushrooms through the oil. Remove and drain. Deep-fry the fish until flaky (illus. 3). Remove and drain.

❹ Retain 3 tablespoons of oil in the wok. Fry the garlic and green onion until fragrant, then add ② , cabbage, pork, mushrooms and fish. Bring to a boil over a high flame. Cover, and simmer until little sauce is left; mix in ③ , then stir in ④ , to thicken, before sprinkling on the sesame oil.

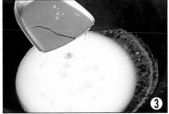

6 人份　Serves 6

奶油白菜

Creamed Cabbage

材料：

大白菜	·················	300公克
中式火腿	·················	60公克
高湯	·················	2 杯
①	奶水 ·················	$\frac{1}{3}$ 杯
	鹽 ·················	$\frac{1}{2}$ 小匙
	味精 ·················	$\frac{1}{4}$ 小匙
②	太白粉、水 ·············	各 1 小匙
雞油	·················	少許

❶白菜洗淨，切3公分長片狀(圖1)，入開水中氽燙至軟，撈起備用。

❷火腿切3×4公分薄片(圖2)，另取一小部分剁成末(約1大匙)備用。

❸高湯2杯、火腿片及白菜均入鍋中，燜煮至湯汁剩約$\frac{1}{3}$時，將材料撈起排盤備用。

❹剩下的湯汁入①料煮開，以②料勾芡，淋上雞油(圖3)拌勻，再淋於白菜上，灑上火腿末即可。

INGREDIENTS:

300 g. ($\frac{2}{3}$ lb.)		nappa cabbage
60 g. (2 oz.)		Chinese style ham
2 c.		chicken broth
①	$\frac{1}{3}$ c.	evaporated milk
	$\frac{1}{2}$ t.	salt
②	1 t. each:	cornstarch, water
Dash		chicken fat

❶ Rinse the cabbage clean and cut into 3 cm. long slices (illus. 1). Par boil until soft. Remove from water for later use.

❷ Cut the ham into 3×4 cm. thin slices (illus. 2). Use a small portion of this ham to mince (about 1 tablespoon).

❸ Place the chicken broth, ham slices, and cabbage in the wok. Simmer, covered, until only one-third of the soup is left. Remove the ham and cabbage to the serving dish.

❹ Bring the remaining soup, with ① added, to a boil. Stir in ②, to thicken, then sprinkle on the chicken fat (illus. 3). Mix evenly, then pour the sauce on the cabbage. Sprinkle on the minced ham.

髮菜豆苗

Black Moss and Pea Leaves

材料：

豆苗	…………………	300公克
髮菜	…………………	10公克
油	…………………	3大匙
①	薑末、葱末、蒜末……	各1小匙
②	水 …………………	¼杯
	酒…………………	1小匙
	鹽 …………………	½小匙
	味精 ………………	¼小匙
③	高湯 ………………	1杯
	鹽 …………………	½小匙
	味精 ………………	¼小匙
	胡椒粉 ……………	少許
④	太白粉、水…………	各1小匙
麻油	…………………	½大匙
酒	…………………	少許

❶豆苗去老纖維（圖１），洗淨；髮菜泡軟（圖２）洗淨，瀝乾水分；均備用。

❷鍋燒熱，入油３大匙，入①料爆香，隨入豆苗及②料拌炒數下，起鍋前灑上少許酒拌勻，盛起置盤。

❸③料煮開，入髮菜（圖３），以小火燜煮至湯汁快收乾，以④料勾芡，起鍋前灑上麻油，置豆苗上即可。

INGREDIENTS:

300 g. (⅔ lb.)		tender pea stalks and leaves
10 g. (⅓ oz.)		dried black moss ("fa tsai")
3 T.		oil
①	1 t. each:	minced-ginger, green onion, garlic
②	¼ c.	water
	1 t.	wine
	½ t.	salt
③	1 c.	chicken broth
	½ t.	salt
	Dash	pepper
④	1 t. each:	cornstarch, water
	½ T.	sesame oil
	Dash	wine

❶ Remove older and tougher parts of pea greens (illus. 1). Wash and drain. Soak the black moss until soft (illus. 2), then rinse and drain.

❷ Heat the wok and add 3 tablespoons of oil. Fry ① until fragrant, then add pea greens as well as ②. Before removing from pan, add a dash of wine. Place on serving plate.

❸ Place ③ in the wok and bring to a boil; then, over a low flame add the black moss (illus. 3). Cover and simmer until sauce is almost gone. Stir in ④ to thicken. Before removing black moss from wok, sprinkle on sesame oil. Black moss is then removed from wok and seated upon the pea greens.

6人份　Serves 6

澎湖絲瓜

Fragrant Loofah

材料：

角瓜(圖1)	600公克
蔥段	8 段
油	4 杯
蝦米	1 大匙
麻油	½ 大匙
蒜片	1 小匙

① 高湯……………………… 1 杯
　 鹽………………………… ⅔ 小匙
　 味精……………………… ¼ 小匙
② 太白粉、水………………各 1 小匙

❶ 角瓜去皮，切3公分長段(圖2)，再直切成寬1公分長形片狀(圖3)；蝦米泡水、洗淨備用。

❷ 鍋燒熱，入油4杯，燒至8分熱(160℃，320°F)，入角瓜過油，撈起備用。

❸ 鍋內留油2大匙，入蔥段及蒜片爆香，再入蝦米、①料及角瓜煮開，改小火燜煮至湯汁剩少許時，以②料勾芡，起鍋前灑上麻油即可。

■ 若角瓜不過油，可以入開水汆燙，但較不香。

INGREDIENTS:

600 g. (1⅓ lb.)	angled loofah (illus. 1) (vegetable sponge)
8 sections	green onion
4 c.	oil
1 T.	small dried shrimp
½ T.	sesame oil
1 t.	garlic slices

① { 1 c. — chicken broth
　 ⅔ t. — salt
② 1 t. each: — cornstarch, water

❶ Remove the skins from the loofah and cut into 3 cm. lengths (illus. 2). Cut again into 1 cm. wide slices (illus. 3). Soak the shrimp until soft, then rinse clean.

❷ Heat the wok and add 4 cups of oil. Heat the oil to 160° C (320° F), before deep-frying the loofah briefly. Remove from the wok.

❸ Retain 2 tablespoons of oil in the wok. Fry the onion and garlic until fragrant, then add shrimp, ① and loofah. Bring to a boil, turn down the flame, and simmer, covered, until only a small amount of sauce remains. Stir in ②, to thicken, then sprinkle on the sesame oil and remove to a serving dish.

■ If you do not wish to deep-fry the loofah, it may be par boiled; however, the taste will not be quite as good.

煎菜脯蛋
Radish and Egg Pancake

材料：

蛋	3 個
蘿蔔乾	100公克
油	$\frac{2}{3}$ 杯
葱末	1 大匙
蒜末	$\frac{1}{2}$ 大匙
① 糖	$\frac{1}{4}$ 小匙
味精	$\frac{1}{8}$ 小匙
鹽、麻油、胡椒粉	各少許

❶蘿蔔乾洗淨、剁碎，泡水10分鐘，瀝乾水分；入熱鍋中炒乾，取出備用。

❷鍋燒熱，入油2大匙，續入蒜末爆香，再入蘿蔔乾及①料拌炒數下，待涼備用。

❸蛋打散，與葱花及蘿蔔乾拌勻；靜置數分鐘，使蘿蔔乾沈至碗底。

❹鍋燒熱，入油$\frac{1}{2}$杯，燒至7分熱(140°C，280°F)，先倒入蛋汁(圖1)，以中火將蛋汁煎至半熟，再倒入蘿蔔乾(圖2)，改小火煎數分鐘，將油倒出來，淋在蘿蔔乾上(圖3)，再將油倒出、菜脯蛋反面；如此反覆二次後，以筷子將中間插數個小洞待中心熟即可。

INGREDIENTS:

3	eggs
100 g. (3½ oz.)	salt-preserved daikon
⅔ c.	oil
1 T.	minced green onion
½ T.	minced garlic
① ¼ t.	sugar
Dash each:	salt, sesame oil, pepper

❶ Rinse the daikon clean and chop. Soak in water for 10 minutes, then remove and drain. Place in wok and stir fry (without oil), until dry. Remove from wok.

❷ Heat the wok and add 2 tablespoons of oil. Fry the garlic until fragrant, then add the daikon and ①; stir-fry briefly. Let this cool.

❸ Beat the eggs, then stir in evenly, the green onion and daikon. Let sit for several minutes, until the daikon settles on the bottom of the bowl.

❹ Heat the wok and add ½ cup of oil. Bring to 140° C (280° F), then pour in the eggs (illus. 1). Over a medium flame cook eggs until half done, then add the daikon (illus. 2). Turn the flame to low and fry for several minutes before pouring off the oil. Pour the oil back in the wok over the daikon (illus. 3). Once again, pour off the oil. Do this two times, before using a chopstick to poke several small holes in the center so that the center will cook throroughly.

6人份　Serves 6

❶

❷

❸

富貴銀耳

Precious White Fungus

材料：

雞胸肉	·························	100公克
白木耳	·························	10公克
草蝦(小)	·························	12隻
鮑魚罐頭	·························	1罐
草菇罐頭	·························	12朵
蛋	·························	6個
葱尾段	·························	24段
雞油	·························	1大匙

①	蛋白	················	½個
	太白粉	················	½小匙
	鹽	················	¼小匙
	味精	················	少許
②	高湯	················	1⅓杯
	鹽	················	¼小匙
	味精	················	少許
③	高湯	················	3杯
	鹽	················	½小匙
	味精	················	¼小匙

❶白木耳泡軟去蒂、洗淨瀝乾；草蝦洗淨、去
腸泥、燙熟、去殼備用。

❷鮑魚切5×3×0.5公分片狀12片；雞胸肉切
絲，入①料拌勻，入開水中氽燙，撈起瀝乾
水分備用。

❸蛋打散，與②料拌勻，以篩網過篩，放入深
盤內，盤中央置一小盆(圖1)；待蒸籠水開
，入蒸籠，以小火蒸10分鐘，待熟取出，拿
去小盆，令深盤中央呈一凹槽(圖2)備用。

❹將鮑魚片排在蒸蛋上(圖3)，再將草菇、葱
尾段、草蝦裝飾在鮑魚周圍；雞胸肉置凹槽
內備用。

❺③料煮開，入銀耳再煮開，盛起，淋在雞絲
上；入蒸籠，再蒸5分鐘即可。

6人份　Serves 6

INGREDIENTS:　　　　　　　　Serves 6

100 g. (3½ oz.)	chicken breast fillets
10 g. (⅓ oz.)	dried white fungus
12	small shrimp
1 can	abalone
12	canned straw mush-rooms
6	eggs
24 sections	green onion tops
1 T.	chicken fat

①	½	egg white
	½ t.	cornstarch
	¼ t.	salt
②	1⅓ c.	chicken broth
	¼ t.	salt
③	3 c.	chicken broth
	½ t.	salt

❶ Soak white fungus and remove stems. Rinse and drain. Rinse the shrimp and devein; boil briefly until cooked. Drain the shrimp and remove shells.

❷ Cut the abalone into 5×3×0.5 cm. slices (12 pieces total). Cut the chicken breast into strips, then mix with ① . Blanch the chicken, then remove and drain.

❸ Beat the eggs before mixing in ② . In order to create a cavity to put the chicken breast in later, place a small bowl in the middle of a deep dish (illus. 1), then add egg mixture. When the water in the steamer begins to boil, place the dish in and steam over a low flame for 10 minutes or until done. Remove the small bowl. A cavity should remain in the middle (illus. 2).

❹ Place abalone on top of the steamed egg (illus. 3). Surround the abalone with straw mushrooms, green onion and shrimp. Place the chicken breast inside the cavity.

❺ Bring ③ to a boil, add white fungus and boil again. Remove this from the wok and sprinkle on top of the chicken. Steam chicken and eggs for 5 more minutes.

①

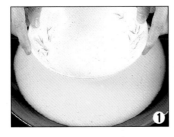
②

③

蟳焗豆腐：作法見第86頁
鐵板豆腐：作法見第87頁
家鄉豆腐：作法見第88頁

Baked Crab Sauce Tofu (p.86)
Fondue Tofu (p.87)
Home-Style Tofu (p.88)

蟳焗豆腐

Baked Crab Sauce Tofu

材料：

蟳肉、絞肉	··················	各80公克
豆腐	··················	2 塊
四季豆	··················	2 條
①	蛋 ·················	$\frac{1}{2}$ 個
	沙拉油 ···········	$\frac{1}{2}$ 杯
	鹽 ·················	$\frac{1}{4}$ 小匙
②	蛋白、太白粉、鹽、味精········	
		各少許
③	高湯 ·············	1 杯
	辣醬（圖 1 ） ·····	1 小匙
	鹽 ·················	$\frac{1}{2}$ 小匙
	味精 ·············	少許
④	太白粉、水 ········	各 2 小匙
	薑汁、麻油 ········	各 1 小匙
	油 ················	少許

❶豆腐共切成8小塊；絞肉入②料拌勻；蟳肉入1小
　匙薑汁拌勻，入蒸籠蒸熟；均備用。

❷四季豆燙熟，切小丁；①料以打蛋器打成沙拉醬
　；均備用。

❸烤盤刷油，排入豆腐；豆腐上先挖去少許豆腐，塞
　入絞肉（圖2），再塗沙拉醬（圖3）；入烤箱，以
　350°C（700°F）烤5～6分鐘，呈金黃色即可。

❹③料煮開，以④料勾芡，入蟳肉及四季豆拌勻，起
　鍋前灑上麻油，淋在豆腐上即可。

■ 如無蟳肉，蟹肉亦可。

INGREDIENTS:

80 g. (2¾ oz.) each:		crab meat, ground pork
2 cakes		tofu
2		string beans
①	½	egg
	½ c.	oil
	¼ t.	salt
②	Dash each:	egg white, cornstarch, salt
③	1 c.	chicken broth
	1 t.	hot sauce (illus. 1)
	½ t.	salt
④	2 t. each:	cornstarch, water
	1 t. each:	ginger juice, sesame oil
	Dash	oil

❶ Cut the tofu into 8 equal pieces. Mix pork and ② . Mix the crab meat and 1 teaspoon of ginger juice, then steam until cooked.

❷ Par boil the string beans and cut into small sections. Use a mixer to beat ① - making mayonnaise.

❸ Brush oil on the inside of a baking dish, then place tofu in flatly. Scoop out a small amount of tofu from each piece and fill with the ground pork mixture (illus. 2). Spread mayonnaise on top (illus. 3). Place in a 350° C (700° F) oven and bake for 5-6 minutes, until just golden brown.

❹ Bring ③ to a boil, add ④ , to thicken, then stir in the crab and beans. Finally, sprinkle on the sesame oil. Pour this sauce on the baked tofu and serve.

鐵板豆腐

Fondue Tofu

材料：

豆腐	1½ 塊
臘肉	20公克
罐頭洋菇片	30公克
青蒜尾段	10公克
油	3 杯
紅辣椒片	2 大匙

①
高湯	1 杯
醬油	1½ 大匙
酒	½ 大匙
冰糖	1 小匙
辣豆瓣醬	½ 小匙
鹽、味精、胡椒粉	各少許

麻油	½ 大匙
酒精火鍋	1 個
酒精塊	1 塊

❶豆腐等切12片；油燒至8分熟（160℃，320℉），入豆腐略炸，撈起備用。

❷青蒜置火鍋內（圖1），上置豆腐（圖2），再灑上臘肉、洋菇片及紅辣椒片備用。

❸①料煮開，起鍋前灑上麻油，淋在豆腐上（圖3），上桌前點著酒精塊即可。

INGREDIENTS:

1½ cakes	tofu
20 g. (⅔ oz.)	sliced Chinese bacon
30 g. (1 oz.)	canned, sliced mush-rooms
10 g. (⅓ oz.)	leek stems
3 c.	oil
2 T.	sliced red chili pepper

①
1 c.	chicken broth
1½ T.	soy sauce
½ T.	wine
1 t.	rock (crystal) sugar
½ t.	hot bean paste
Dash each:	salt, pepper

½ T.	sesame oil

foundue pot and burner with liquid heat

❶ Cut the tofu into 12 equal pieces. Heat the oil to 160° C (320 ° F). Fry the tofu until just browned.

❷ Place the leeks in the bottom of the fondue (illus. 1). Place tofu on this (illus. 2), then sprinkle on the bacon, mushrooms, and red chili pepper.

❸ Bring ① to a boil. Right before removing from pan sprinkle on sesame oil. Pour this sauce on tofu (illus. 3). Light burner just before bringing the fondue to the table.

家鄉豆腐

Home-Style Tofu

材料：

豆腐	……………………	1½塊
里肌肉	……………………	60公克
青蒜尾(圖1)段	……………	¼ 杯
油	……………………	7大匙

① { 黑豆豉(洗淨，圖2)、紅辣椒絲
　　…………………… 各 2 大匙
蒜片 …………………… 1½ 小匙

② { 蛋白 …………………… ¼ 個
太白粉 …………………… ¾ 小匙
醬油 …………………… ½ 小匙
味精 …………………… 少許

③ { 高湯 …………………… 1 杯
醬油 …………………… 1½ 大匙
糖、胡椒粉 …………… 各少許

④ 太白粉、水 …………… 各1½ 小匙

麻油 …………………… 1½ 小匙

❶里肌肉切絲，入②料拌勻；豆腐切1公分寬條狀備用。

❷鍋燒熱，入油3大匙燒熱，先入里肌肉炒熟盛起；續入油2大匙燒熱，再入豆腐煎至金黃色備用。

❸鍋燒熱，入油2大匙，入①料爆香，續入③料煮開，以④料勾芡，再入豆腐及肉絲(圖3)拌勻，起鍋前灑上麻油及青蒜尾段即可。

■黑豆豉處理方式同蔭豉鮮蚵(見第15頁)。

INGREDIENTS:

1½ cakes	tofu	
60 g. (2 oz.)	pork tenderloin	
¼ c.	leek stem sections (illus. 1)	
7 T.	oil	

① { 2 T. each: cleaned (fermented) black beans (illus. 2), shredded red chili pepper
1½ t. sliced garlic

② { ¼ egg white
¾ t. cornstarch
½ t. soy sauce

③ { 1 c. chicken broth
1½ T. soy sauce
Dash each: sugar, pepper

④ 1½ t. each: cornstarch, water

1½ t. sesame oil

❶ Julienne the pork and mix with ② . Cut the tofu into 1 cm. wide strips.

❷ Heat the wok and add 3 tablespoons of oil. Add the pork and fry until done. Remove and drain. Add 2 more tablespoons oil to the wok and fry the tofu until golden brown. Remove and drain.

❸ Heat the wok and add 2 tablespoons of oil; stir fry ① until fragrant, then add ③ and bring to a boil. Stir in ④, to thicken, then add tofu and pork (illus. 3). Sprinkle on the sesame oil and stir in the leek stems just before removal to serving platter.

■ Method for cleaning the black beans is found in "Oysters with Black Bean Sauce" (page 15) recipe.

6 人份　Serves 6

炸豆腐　Fried Tofu

材料：

豆腐	……………………	1½塊
油	……………………	3杯

①

醬油 ………………	1½大匙
香菜末、葱末 ………	各2小匙
蒜末、辣椒末、糖、黑醋………	
……………………	各¾小匙
味精、胡椒粉……………	各少許

❶豆腐切6小長方塊，再對切成三角形(圖1)；①料拌匀(圖2)；均備用。

❷鍋燒熱，入油3杯燒至9分熱(180℃，360°F)，入豆腐炸至金黃色，撈起瀝油(圖3)排盤。

❸食時沾①料即可。

INGREDIENTS:

1½ cakes	tofu
3 c.	oil

	1½ T.	soy sauce
	2 t. each:	minced-coriander, green onion
①	¾ t. each:	minced-garlic, red chili pepper, sugar, dark vinegar
	Dash	pepper

❶ Cut the tofu into 6 rectangles. Cut again slantwise to create triangles (illus. 1). Mix ① evenly together (illus. 2) - this is the dip.

❷ Heat the wok and add 3 cups of oil. Heat to 180° C (360° F). Fry tofu until golden brown. Drain and remove to platter (illus. 3).

❸ Dip tofu in ① when eating.

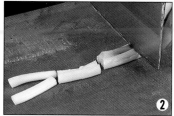

6 人份　Serves 6

干煎豆腐

Sautéed Bean Curd

材料：
豆腐……………………………1塊
蔥……………………………2支
油……………………………2杯
① {
高湯…………………………2大匙
醬油、麻油、酒……………
……………………………各1小匙
糖……………………………½小匙
味精…………………………少許
}

❶豆腐切8片(圖1)；蔥切5公分長段(圖2)備用。
❷油燒至8分熱(160℃，320℉)，入豆腐煎炸至金黃色(圖3)，撈起備用。
❸鍋內留油2大匙，先入蔥段爆香，再入①料及豆腐，以小火燜煮至湯汁剩⅓即可。

INGREDIENTS:

1 cake	tofu (bean curd)	
2 stems	green onion	
2 c.	oil	
① {	2 T.	chicken broth
	1 t. each:	soy sauce, sesame oil, wine
	½ t.	sugar

❶ Cut the tofu into 8 pieces (illus. 1). Cut the onion into 5 cm. lengths (illus. 2).

❷ Heat oil to 160° C (320° F), then add the tofu and fry until golden brown (illus. 3). Remove from wok.

❸ Remove all but 2 tablespoons of oil from the pan. First add the onion and cook until it becomes fragrant. Add the tofu and ① . Use a low flame to cook, covered, until only one-third of the sauce remains.

6 人份　Serves 6

金針雞湯

Lily Bud Chicken Soup

材料：
半土雞	……………………	450公克
金針	……………………	40公克
① 水	……………………	5 杯
酒	……………………	1 大匙
鹽	……………………	1 小匙
味精	……………………	¼ 小匙

❶半土雞洗淨，剁成24等份；入開水中氽燙去血水，撈起漂涼備用。

❷金針洗淨，每支均打結（圖1），泡軟備用。

❸取一燉碗，將雞塊整齊地排入碗中（圖2）再入金針（圖3）及①料，待蒸籠水開，將燉碗放入蒸籠，大火蒸40分鐘即可。

INGREDIENTS:
450 g. (1 lb.)		chicken
40 g. (1⅓ oz.)		dried lily buds
①	5 c.	water
	1 T.	wine
	1 t.	salt

❶ Rinse the chicken clean and cut into 24 equal pieces. Blanch in boiling water to rid chicken of blood. Drain and cool chicken.

❷ Rinse lily buds clean and tie each in a knot (illus. 1). Soak until soft.

❸ Use a heatproof bowl. Place chicken in bowl neatly (illus. 2). Add lily buds (illus. 3) and ① . When water in steamer boils, place bowl in. Over a high flame steam for 40 minutes.

一品燉雞

材料：

半土雞	600公克
大白菜	240公克
蹄筋(圖1)、罐頭鮑魚、罐頭松茸	各120公克
熟竹筍	100公克
中式火腿	80公克
豌豆莢	10公克
干貝	6個
豆腐	1塊
香菇	3朵
紅蘿蔔	1片

①
高湯	6杯
酒	½大匙
鹽	1小匙
味精	¼小匙

玻璃紙 ………… 1張

❶半土雞洗淨，剁成3×5公分塊狀；蹄筋、鮑魚、松茸、竹筍、火腿切相同大小薄片；豆腐切菱形大丁狀(圖2)；香菇泡軟、去蒂、切片；干貝洗淨備用。

❷雞塊入開水中氽燙去血水，撈起洗淨；白菜洗淨切段，豌豆莢洗淨、去老纖維，均入開水燙軟，撈起瀝乾備用。

❸取一深盤，入豆腐墊底，中央置雞塊；以雞塊為中心，入白菜將深盤分成4等份(圖3)，豌豆莢、竹筍片、火腿片及香菇片置大白菜上裝飾；再分別將蹄筋、松茸、鮑魚、干貝擺入各空格內；輕輕倒入①料，中間以紅蘿蔔片點綴，上蓋玻璃紙備用。

❹蒸籠的水燒開，入❸項材料，以大火蒸40分鐘即可。

6人份　Serves 6

First-Class Stewed Chicken Soup

INGREDIENTS:

600 g. (1⅓ lb.)	chicken
240 g. (½ lb.)	nappa cabbage
120 g. (¼ lb.) each:	pork tendons (illus. 1), canned abalone, canned matsutake mushrooms
100 g. (3½ oz.)	canned bamboo shoots
80 g. (2¾ oz.)	Chinese style ham
10 g. (⅓ oz.)	snow peas
6	dried scallops
1 cake	tofu
3	dried black mushrooms
1 slice	carrot

①
6 c.	chicken broth
½ T.	wine
1 t.	salt

1 sheet	cellophane

❶ Rinse the chicken clean and chop into 3×5 cm. pieces. Cut the pork tendons, abalone, matsutake mushrooms, bamboo and ham into equally-sized thin slices. Cut the tofu into large diamond-shaped pieces (illus. 2). Soak the black mushrooms until soft. Remove stems and slice. Wash and drain the scallops.

❷ Blanch the chicken, rinse, and drain. Wash and cut the cabbage into even sections. Wash the snow peas and remove strings. Blanch cabbage and peas, then drain.

❸ Use a deep dish and place tofu in the bottom. Place chicken on top of tofu in the center. Divide the cabbage into 4 equal amounts and use to divide the dish into 4 sections (illus. 3). Place snow peas, bamboo, ham and black mushrooms on top of cabbage. Fill one section with pork tendons, another with matsutake mushrooms, another with abalone and the last with scallops. Gently pour on ① . Place the carrot slice on the middle top. Cover dish with cellophane.

❹ When water begins to boil in steamer, place the dish in. Steam for 40 minutes over a high flame.

93

蛋衣蝦卷

Egg-Dressed Shrimp Rolls

材料：

蘆蝦仁 …………………………	260公克
豆苗 ……………………………	240公克
蛋……………………………………	5個
紫菜皮 ………………………………	1½張
麵糊…………………………………	2 大匙
葱末 …………………………………	1 大匙

①
- 蛋白 …………………………… ⅓個
- 酒、麻油、太白粉…… 各1小匙
- 鹽、味精 ……………… 各⅓小匙

②
- 高湯 ……………………………… 5杯
- 酒………………………………… ½大匙
- 鹽 ………………………………… 1小匙
- 味精 ……………………………… 少許

香菜末、胡椒粉、麻油……… 各少許
竹簾…………………………………… 1個

❶蘆蝦仁去腸泥、洗淨，以乾布擦乾(圖1)，
再以刀背拍碎，入1料拌勻，即爲蝦泥，分
成3等份備用。

❷蛋打散成蛋液，以平底鍋煎成3張直徑約20
公分之圓形蛋皮。紫菜皮1張對切成兩半備
用。

❸竹簾上置1張蛋皮，再置紫菜皮半張，再放
1份蝦泥餡(圖2)，捲成長條狀(圖3)，接
口處以麵糊黏牢，共做3份；待蒸籠的水開
，將蝦卷放入蒸籠，大火蒸6分鐘，取出切
1.5公分斜片備用。

❹豆苗洗淨，放入大碗中，將蝦卷置於豆苗上
；2料煮開，沖入大碗中，灑上葱末、香菜
、胡椒粉、麻油即可。

INGREDIENTS:

260 g. (9 oz.)	medium-sized shelled prawns or shrimp
240 g. (8½ oz.)	pea leaves and top stems
5	eggs
1½	laver seaweed sheets ("nori")
2 T.	flour paste
1 T.	minced green onion

①
⅓	egg white
1 t. each:	wine, sesame oil, cornstarch
⅓ t.	salt

②
5 c.	chicken broth
½ T.	wine
1 t.	salt

Dash each:	minced coriander, pepper, sesame oil
1	bamboo mat

❶ Devein, clean and dry the shrimp (illus. 1), then use the knife to pound the shrimp into small pieces. Mix the mashed shrimp with ① and divide into 3 portions. This is the shrimp filling.

❷ Beat the eggs until blended. Divide, and in a flat-bottomed pan, fry into 3 round egg sheets, of about 20 cms. in diameter. Cut the whole seaweed sheet in half.

❸ Place one egg sheet on the bamboo mat, then one sheet of seaweed, and finally, a portion of the shrimp filling (illus. 2). Roll into a long cylinder (illus. 3). Seal with the flour paste. Make 3. Place the rolls in the steamer basket, and over a high flame, steam for 6 minutes. Remove and cut into approximately 1.5 cm. diagonal slices.

❹ Rinse the pea greens and place in a large bowl. Put the shrimp rolls on top of the pea greens. Bring ② to a boil, and pour into the bowl. Sprinkle on the green onion, coriander, pepper, and sesame oil, then serve.

6人份　Serves 6

螺肉蒜湯

Garlic Escargot′ Fondue

材料：

螺肉罐頭(圖1)	1罐
芹菜、青蒜	各150公克
乾魷魚	100公克
後腿肉	80公克
香菇	20公克
高湯	5杯
油	2大匙

① 蛋白 $\frac{1}{4}$個
太白粉 1小匙
鹽、味精 各$\frac{1}{8}$小匙

② 螺肉罐頭汁 $\frac{1}{2}$杯
鹽 1小匙
味精 $\frac{1}{4}$小匙

酒精火鍋	1個
酒精塊	1塊

❶芹菜、青蒜洗淨，均切段；乾魷魚以剪刀剪成1×5公分長條(圖2)洗淨；後腿肉切薄片，入①料拌勻；香菇泡軟、去蒂、切片；均備用。

❷水燒開，分別入腿肉及魷魚汆燙，撈起備用。

❸鍋燒熱，入油2大匙，再入芹菜及青蒜段爆香，續入高湯5杯煮開，撈起芹菜及青蒜段，置火鍋碗內(圖3)；再將後腿肉、螺肉、香菇、及魷魚依次置芹菜及青蒜段上；湯汁備用。

❹❸項湯汁入②料再煮開，倒入火鍋碗內，上桌前點著酒精塊即可。

INGREDIENTS:

1 can	snails (illus. 1)
150 g. (⅓ lb.) each:	Chinese celery, leeks
100 g. (3½ oz.)	dried squid
80 g. (2¾ oz.)	pork shank
20 g. (⅔ oz.)	dried black mushrooms
5 c.	chicken broth
2 T.	oil

① ¼ egg white
1 t. cornstarch
⅛ t. salt

② ½ c. canned snail marinade
1 t. salt

fondue pot and burner with liquid heat

❶ Clean, then cut the celery and leeks into equal sections. Cut the squid into 1×5 cm. long strips (illus. 2). Rinse clean. Cut the pork into thin slices and mix with ① . Soak the mushrooms, remove stems and slice.

❷ Separately scald the pork and squid. Remove and drain for later use.

❸ Heat the wok and add 2 tablespoons of oil. Cook until fragrant the celery and leeks. Add the chicken broth and bring to a boil. Remove celery and leeks and place in fondue (illus. 3). Place pork, snails, mushrooms and squid on top of celery and leeks. Retain the soup broth for use in step ❹ .

❹ Add ② to the soup broth from step ❸ and bring to a boil. Pour broth into fondue pot. Light burner just before bringing fondue to the table.

6人份　Serves 6

蛤蜊冬瓜濃

Clam and Winter Melon Soup

材料：

蛤蜊	…………………	600公克
冬瓜	…………………	240公克
中式火腿、洋菇、紅蘿蔔	…	各40公克
嫩薑片	…………………	10公克
香菇	…………………	4朵

①	高湯	…………………	3杯
	酒	…………………	1大匙
	鹽	…………………	½小匙
	味精	…………………	¼小匙
	胡椒粉	…………………	少許
②	太白粉、水	…………	各2大匙
水		…………………	4杯
麻油		…………………	少許

❶蛤蜊洗淨、吐砂。水燒開，入蛤蜊汆燙一下，待蛤蜊張口(圖1)，關火，取肉去殼；湯汁留下3杯備用。

❷冬瓜去皮、去籽，切丁並加1杯水，入果汁機打成泥狀(圖2)備用。

❸香菇泡軟、洋菇洗淨，均去蒂、切片；中式火腿切片(圖3)；紅蘿蔔亦切片；均入開水中汆燙，撈起漂涼備用。

❹①料及蛤蜊湯3杯及冬瓜泥煮開，隨入火腿、香菇、紅蘿蔔、洋菇、嫩薑片再煮開，以②料勾芡，並拌入蛤蜊肉，立刻關火；起鍋前灑上麻油即可。

INGREDIENTS:

600 g. (1⅓ lb.)		clams
240 g. (8½ oz.)		winter melon
40 g. (1⅓ oz.) each:		Chinese style ham, mushrooms, carrot
10 g. (⅓ oz.)		sliced young ginger
4		dried black mushrooms
①	3 c.	chicken broth
	1 T.	wine
	½ t.	salt
	Dash	pepper
②	2 T. each:	cornstarch, water
4 c.		water
Dash		sesame oil

❶ Clean clams (rinse and put in 1 quart water with 1 t. salt for several hours so they will release their sand). Boil in 4 cups water until their shells open (illus. 1). Turn off and retain 3 cups of the water. Remove clams and clam meat from shells.

❷ Remove skin and seeds of winter melon. Cut into even pieces. With 1 cup of water place melon in blender and purée (illus. 2).

❸ Soak the black mushrooms until soft. Clean mushrooms. Remove stems of black mushrooms and mushrooms, then slice. Slice ham (illus. 3) and carrot. Parboil these, drain and let cool.

❹ Bring ① , 3 cups of soup stock from step ❶ , and winter melon puree to a boil. Add ham, black mushrooms, carrot, mushrooms and ginger. Bring again to a boil, then thicken with ② . Fold in clam meat and immediately turn off burner. Right before removing to serving bowl sprinkle on sesame oil.

6人份　Serves 6

6 人份　Serves 6

蕃茄排骨湯

Tomato and Pork Rib Soup

材料：

小排骨	480公克
蕃茄	240公克
肉醬罐頭(圖1)	½ 杯
水	6 杯

① ┌ 酒 1 大匙
　├ 鹽 ½ 小匙
　└ 味精 ¼ 小匙

❶排骨剁3×3公分塊狀(圖2)，入開水中氽燙去血水，撈起；蕃茄去蒂，切滾刀塊(圖3)備用。

❷水6杯煮開，入排骨、蕃茄及肉醬，再煮開，以中火續煮約15分鐘，入①料拌勻即可。

INGREDIENTS:

480 g. (1 lb. 1 oz.)	pork ribs
240 g. (8½ oz.)	tomatoes
½ c.	canned pork paste or minced-meat (illus. 1)
6 c.	water

① ┌ 1 T. — wine
　└ ½ t. — salt

❶ Chop the pork ribs into 3×3 cm. pieces (illus. 2). Scald, then remove from the water. Remove the tomato stems and cut the tomatoes into irregular pieces (illus. 3).

❷ Bring 6 cups of water to a boil. Add the pork ribs, tomatoes and pork paste. Bring this to a boil, then simmer, over a medium flame, for 15 minutes. Stir in ① , then serve.

髮菜濃湯

Forest Soup

材料：

熟筍絲	80公克
里肌肉	40公克
髮菜、中式火腿末	各10公克
高湯	5杯
芹菜末	1 大匙

① 蛋白 …… 1 小匙
太白粉 …… $\frac{1}{2}$ 小匙
鹽 …… $\frac{1}{4}$ 小匙
味精 …… 少許

② 鹽、黑醋 …… 各 1 小匙
味精、胡椒粉 …… 各少許

③ 太白粉、水 …… 各 2 大匙

❶髮菜泡軟、洗淨；里肌肉切細絲，入①料拌勻（圖1）備用。

❷高湯煮開，入髮菜、筍絲、肉絲、火腿末（圖2），再煮開，入②料拌勻，以③料勾芡（圖3），起鍋前灑上芹菜末即可。

INGREDIENTS:

80 g. (2¾ oz.)	julienned, canned bamboo shoots
40 g. (1⅓ oz.)	pork tenderloin
10 g. (⅓ oz.) each:	dried black moss ("fa tsai"), minced Chinese style ham
5 c.	chicken broth
1 T.	Chinese celery

① 1 t.   egg white
½ t.   cornstarch
¼ t.   salt

② 1 t.   salt, dark vinegar
Dash   pepper

③ 2 T. each: cornstarch, water

❶ Soak the black moss until soft and then rinse clean. Cut the pork into fine strips and mix with ① (illus. 1).

❷ Boil the broth, then add black moss, bamboo, pork and ham (illus. 2), and once again bring to a boil. Mix in ② , then thicken with ③ (illus. 3). Sprinkle celery onto top of soup right before removing from pan.

101

鷄絲濃湯

Chicken Julienne Soup

材料：

荸薺、雞胸肉	⋯⋯⋯⋯⋯⋯	各80公克
濕木耳(圖1)	⋯⋯⋯⋯⋯	50公克
餛飩皮	⋯⋯⋯⋯⋯⋯	20公克
蛋白	⋯⋯⋯⋯⋯⋯	1個
高湯	⋯⋯⋯⋯⋯⋯	5杯
油	⋯⋯⋯⋯⋯⋯	1杯
葱末	⋯⋯⋯⋯⋯⋯	1大匙

①	鹽	⋯⋯⋯⋯⋯	1小匙
	味精	⋯⋯⋯⋯⋯	$\frac{1}{4}$小匙
	胡椒粉	⋯⋯⋯⋯⋯	$\frac{1}{8}$小匙
②	太白粉、水	⋯⋯⋯⋯	各2大匙

❶荸薺、餛飩皮、木耳均切細絲；雞胸肉煮熟亦撕成絲(圖2)備用。

❷油燒至8分熱（160°C，320°F），入餛飩皮炸至金黃色(圖3)，撈起瀝油備用。

❸高湯煮開，入木耳絲、荸薺絲、雞絲煮開，再入①料拌勻，以②料勾芡，再倒入蛋白拌勻，起鍋前灑上葱末及餛飩皮即可。

INGREDIENTS:

80 g. (2¾ oz.) each:	water chestnuts, chicken breast fillets
50 g. (1¾ oz.)	soaked dried wood ears (illus. 1)
20 g. (⅔ oz.)	won ton skins
1	egg white
5 c.	chicken broth
1 c.	oil
1 T.	minced green onion
① { 1 t.	salt
⅛ t.	pepper
② 2 T. each:	cornstarch, water

❶ Slice water chestnuts, won ton skins and wood ears into fine strips. Boil the chicken until cooked then tear into fine strips (illus. 2)

❷ Heat oil to 160° C (320° F), add won ton skins and fry until golden brown (illus. 3). Remove from oil and drain.

❸ Bring the broth to a boil before mixing in wood ears, water chestnuts, chicken. Bring this to a boil, then add ① . Thicken with ② . Pour egg white slowly into soup, sirring gently as you do. Green onion and won ton skins are sprinkled on top of the soup mixture right before removal from pan.

6 人份　Serves 6

花瓜雞湯

材料：
半土雞	450公克
花瓜罐(圖1)	1 罐
水	5 杯
花瓜汁	1 大匙
鹽	½ 小匙
味精	少許

❶將雞洗淨，切5×4公分大小(圖2)，入開水中汆燙，撈起漂涼(圖3)備用。

❷將雞塊、花瓜、花瓜汁及水入鍋煮開，續煮30分鐘，入味精拌勻即可。

Pickled Cucumber Chicken Soup

INGREDIENTS:
450 g. (1 lb.)	chicken
1 can	canned pickled cucumbers (illus. 1)
5 c.	water
1 T.	cucumber marinade (retained from canned cucumbers)
½ t.	salt

❶ Rinse the chicken clean and cut into 5×4 cm. pieces (illus. 2). Blanch, then remove and cool (illus. 3).

❷ Place chicken, cucumber, cucumber marinade and water in pan and bring to a boil. Simmer for 30 minutes.

103

筒仔米糕：作法見第106頁
粽　　子：作法見第107頁
蚵仔麵線：作法見第108頁

Bamboo Cup Rice Pudding (p.106)
Jungdz (p.107)
Oyster Noodle Strings (p.108)

1 2 人份 Serves 12

筒仔米糕

Bamboo Cup Rice Pudding

材料：

長糯米	………480公克		醬油	…………1 大匙
五花肉	………200公克		酒	…………1 小匙
熟花生、魚鬆（圖1）	…… ①		糖、冰糖	…各 ½ 小匙
	…各80公克		味精	… ¼ 小匙
香菇絲	…………30公克		胡椒粉	………少許
香菜末	… ½ 杯		高湯	…………1 杯
油葱酥	… ¼ 杯		醬油	…………3 大匙
油	…… 4 大匙	②	酒	… ½ 大匙
竹筒	…………12個		味精、冰糖	………
玻璃紙（10×10公分）	……			…各 ¼ 小匙
	…………12張		胡椒粉	………少許

❶ 長糯米洗淨，泡水4小時，瀝乾水分；蒸籠內墊一紗布，長糯米置其上舖平，上面噴灑少許水，待蒸籠水開，入蒸籠，大火蒸30分鐘，待熟取出備用。

❷ 五花肉切12塊，入①料拌匀，醃約10分鐘，待蒸籠水開，入蒸籠，蒸約30分鐘，取出備用。

❸ 鍋燒熱，入油4大匙，續入香菇絲爆香，隨入花生及②料拌匀，再入糯米飯及油葱酥拌匀，即爲油飯，分成12等份備用。

❹ 取一竹筒，先入1份肉，再入1份油飯（圖2），壓緊，上蓋1張玻璃紙（圖3），共做12份；待蒸籠水開，入蒸籠，以大火蒸20分鐘，取出倒扣盤中，上面以香菜末及魚鬆裝飾即可。

■ 食時可沾甜辣醬。

■ 米糕上亦可以肉鬆裝飾。

INGREDIENTS:

480 g. (1 lb. 1 oz.)	long-grained glutinous rice
200 g. (7 oz.)	uncured bacon meat
80 g. (2¾ oz.) each:	cooked peanuts, fish fiber (illus. 1)
30 g. (1 oz.)	julienned black mushroom
½ c.	minced coriander
¼ c.	fried shallot flakes
4 T.	oil
12	bamboo cups
12 sheets (10×10 cm.)	cellophane

①	1 T.	soy sauce
	1 t.	wine
	½ t. each:	sugar, rock (crystal) sugar
	Dash	pepper
②	1 c.	chicken broth
	3 T.	soy sauce
	½ T.	wine
	¼ t.	rock (crystal) sugar
	Dash	pepper

❶ Rinse the rice until the water runs clear, then soak for 4 hours. Drain. Place a piece of cheesecloth in the bottom of the steamer basket. Add rice and flatten out, then splash with a little water. Steam for 30 minutes, until cooked, over a high flame. Remove.

❷ Cut meat into 12 large pieces. Mix evenly with ① and marinate for about 10 minutes. Steam for 30 minutes. Remove.

❸ Heat the wok and add 4 tablespoons oil. Fry mushroom until fragrant, then add peanuts and ② , mixing evenly. Add the rice and shallot; again, mix evenly. This is "oily rice." Divide into 12 equal portions.

❹ In each bamboo cup first add 1 portion of meat, then 1 portion of "oily rice" (illus. 2). Press this down and cover with a piece of cellophane (illus. 3). Steam bamboo cups over a high flame for 20 minutes. Remove, turn upside down and tap, to release pudding over serving plate. Sprinkle on minced coriander and fish fiber as a decorative condiment.

■ Dip in sweet chili sauce.

粽　子

Jungdz

材料：

長糯米	480公克
五花肉	60公克
蝦米	20公克
栗子	6 粒
香菇	4 朵
生鹹蛋黃	3 個
油葱酥	4 大匙
竹葉	12片
油	1 杯

① 醬油……4 大匙
　糖……1 小匙
　麻油……½ 小匙
　鹽……¼ 小匙
　味精……⅛ 小匙
　胡椒粉……少許

棉繩……6 條

❶竹葉泡軟，入開水中汆燙，撈起洗淨，瀝乾水分；長糯米泡軟蒸熟（作法見筒仔米糕，第106頁）備用。

❷五花肉切大丁；蝦米洗淨；香菇泡軟、去蒂切片；鹹蛋黃均對切成半；栗子洗淨泡軟、去殼，入熱油中，炸呈金黃色，撈起，再入蒸籠蒸軟；均備用。

❸鍋燒熱，入油4 大匙，續入蝦米、五花肉丁、香菇片爆香，再入①料燜煮數分鐘；將材料撈起，拌入2 大匙油葱酥爲餡，分成6 等份；湯汁備用。

❹將糯米飯與❸之湯汁及2 大匙油葱酥拌勻爲油飯，亦分成6 等份備用。

❺取二片竹葉重疊，折成漏斗狀（圖1），上置½ 份油飯（圖2），再置1 份餡及半個鹹蛋黃，蓋上½ 份油飯，包成粽子狀，以棉繩綁緊（圖3），共做6 個；待蒸籠的水開，入蒸籠，大火蒸25分鐘即可。

INGREDIENTS:

480 g. (1 lb. 1 oz.)	long-grained glutinous rice
60 g. (2 oz.)	uncured bacon meat
20 g. (⅔ oz.)	small dried shrimp
6	chestnuts
4	dried black mushrooms
3	raw salt-preserved egg yolks
4 T.	fried shallot flakes
12	bamboo leaves
1 c.	oil

① 4 T. — soy sauce
　1 t. — sugar
　½ t. — sesame oil
　¼ t. — salt
　Dash — pepper

6 lengths — cotton string

❶ Soak the bamboo leaves until soft, then scald in water. Drain. Soak the rice and cook (see "Bamboo Cup Rice Pudding" page 106).

❷ Cut the meat into large pieces. Rinse the shrimp clean. Soak the mushrooms, remove stems and slice. Cut the egg yolks into even halves. Soak the chestnuts until soft, remove the shells, then in hot oil deep fry until golden brown. Finally, steam the chestnuts until soft.

❸ Heat the wok and add 4 tablespoons oil. Add the shrimp, meat, mushrooms and fry until fragrant. Add ① ; cover and simmer for a few minutes. Remove ingredients from wok and stir in 2 tablespoons of shallots. Divide into 6 portions. Retain the sauce.

❹ Mix evenly the rice, sauce from step ❸ , and 2 tablespoons of shallots. This is "oily rice." Divide into 6 portions.

❺ Pick up 2 bamboo leaves and overlap. Fold into a conical shape (illus. 1). Place ½ of 1 portion "oily rice" in the cup formed (illus. 2), then place in 1 portion filling from step ❸ and half a salty egg. Cover this with the remaining ½ portion of "oily rice." Fold the leaves over and around to form a "jungdz," then tie tightly (illus. 3). There should be 6 "jungdz" altogether. When the water in the steamer boils, place the "jungdz" in and steam over a high flame for 25 minutes.

蚵仔麵線

Oyster Noodle Strings

材料：

大腸	200公克
紅麵線	160公克
生蚵、熟筍絲	各80公克
木耳絲	40公克
柴魚	$\frac{1}{2}$杯
紅蔥酥	$\frac{1}{3}$杯
油	2大匙

①	高湯	6杯
	醬油	2大匙
	麻油	1大匙
	鹽	$\frac{1}{2}$小匙
	味精、糖	各$\frac{1}{4}$小匙
②	太白粉、水	各2大匙

❶大腸以剪刀剪去油脂（圖1），入開水中汆燙一下，取出，翻出內面（圖2），以刀子刮去黏稠（圖3），洗淨，切小丁；鍋燒熱，入油2大匙，再入大腸燜炒數分鐘，取出，再洗淨，瀝乾水分備用。

❷紅麵線切8公分長段；生蚵洗淨，瀝乾水分，入1大匙太白粉拌勻，再入開水中汆燙一下，撈起備用。

❸①料煮開，入筍絲、木耳絲、柴魚、麵線、大腸再煮開，以小火慢煮約15分鐘，以②料勾芡，拌入生蚵即可。

■食時隨個人口味，可加香菜末、辣油、蒜末、醬油等調味料。

■若不敢吃大腸，可不加大腸，①料煮開後，加2大匙豬油即可。

INGREDIENTS:

200 g. (7 oz.)	intestines
160 g. (5½ oz.)	red noodle strings
80 g. (2¾ oz.) each:	oysters, julienned, canned bamboo shoots
40 g. (1⅓ oz.)	wood ears (edible tree fungus)
½ c.	dried fish flakes
⅓ c.	fried shallot flakes
2 T.	oil

①	6 c.	chicken broth
	2 T.	soy sauce
	1 T.	sesame oil
	½ t.	salt
	¼ t.	sugar
②	2 T. each:	cornstarch, water

❶ Remove fat from intestines using a knife (illus. 1). Blanch the intestines in boiling water and remove. Turn inside out (illus. 2). Use a knife to scrape clean (illus. 3). Rinse clean and cut the intestines into small pieces. Then, heat the pan and add 2 tablespoons of oil. Add the intestines, cover, and cook for a few minutes; remove them and rinse clean, then drain.

❷ Cut the noodle strings into lengths of 8 centimeters. Clean the oysters and drain well before mixing 1 tablespoon of cornstarch with them. Scald oysters in boiling water, then drain.

❸ Place ① in the pan. When it comes to a boil, add bamboo, wood ear, fish, noodles and intestines. Let this come to a boil again, then simmer for 15 minutes. Stir in ② , to thicken the soup mixture. Add oysters to the soup and cook until done.

■ Condiments may be added such as: minced coriander, chili oil, minced garlic, soy sauce or any other spice you enjoy.

■ If you dislike intestines, it is not necessary to use them. Instead, add 2 tablespoons of lard when ① comes to a boil.

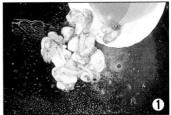

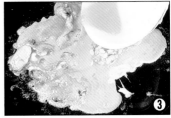

6人份　Serves 6

蚵仔煎

材料：

生蚵	480公克
小白菜或茼蒿	240公克
蛋	6個
油	1杯

① { 水 ⋯⋯⋯⋯⋯⋯⋯⋯1½杯
地瓜粉⋯⋯⋯⋯⋯⋯⋯¾杯
鹽⋯⋯⋯⋯⋯⋯⋯⋯⋯1½小匙
味精⋯⋯⋯⋯⋯⋯⋯⋯少許 }

❶生蚵洗淨，瀝乾水分；蛋打散；各分成6份備用。
❷小白菜洗淨切段，分成6份；①料拌勻備用。
❸平底鍋燒熱，入油3大匙，再入1份生蚵煎半熟（圖1），續入7大匙①料煎半熟（圖2），隨入1份蛋液（圖3）及小白菜置其上，翻面再煎2分鐘即可；共做6份。
■食時可沾甜辣醬。

Oyster Pan Fritters

INGREDIENTS:

480 g (1 lb. 1 oz.) oysters
240 g (8½ oz.) white Chinese cabbage, "tang hau tsai," or other green vegetable
6 eggs
1 c. oil
① { 1½ c. water
¾ c. sweet potato powder
1½ t. salt }

❶ Rinse the oysters clean. Drain. Beat the egg. Separately divide into 6 portions in preparation for use.
❷ Clean, then cut, the vegetable into even sections. Divide into 6 portions. Mix the ingredients from ① together.
❸ Heat a flat-bottomed pan and add 3 tablespoons oil. When the oil is thoroughly heated, add 1 portion of oysters and cook them until half done (illus. 1). Add 7 tablespoons of ① . When this is also half-cooked (illus. 2), add 1 portion each of egg (illus. 3) and vegetable to the top. Turn the fritter over and cook for 2 more minutes. Makes 6 individual fritters.
■ Sweet chili sauce may be used as a dipping sauce.

八寶糯米卷

Eight Treasure Glutinous Rice Rolls

材料：

長糯米	················	300公克
豆皮	················	1½張
油	················	5 杯

① 多瓜糖(圖1)、桔餅(圖2)、蜜餞(圖3)、葡萄乾 …各40公克
花生粉 ················ 20公克

② 糖 ················ 2 大匙
猪油 ················ 1 大匙

③ 麵粉、水 ············ 各1½ 大匙

竹簾 ················ 1 個

❶ 長糯米泡軟蒸熟(作法見筒仔米糕，第106頁)，拌入 ② 料，分成 3 等份備用。

❷ 豆皮一張對切成 2 小張，共 3 小張。① 料中冬瓜糖、桔餅及蜜餞均切丁，再將 ① 料分成 3 等份備用。

❸ 取一小張豆皮放竹簾上，上置 1 份糯米飯鋪平，再將 1 份 ① 料置中間，包捲成長條筒狀，接口處以 ③ 料黏緊，共做 3 份備用。

❹ 將油燒 5 分熱(100°C，200°F)，入糯米卷，大火炸至金黃色，撈起瀝油，切 3 公分長段即可。

INGREDIENTS:

300 g. (⅔ lb.)		long-grained glutinous rice
1½ sheets		bean curd skins
5 c.		oil
①	40 g. (1⅓ oz.) each:	candied winter melon (illus. 1), candied kumquat (illus. 2), raisins, preserved or candied fruits of choice - prunes, mangoes, and red plums are shown (illus. 3)
	20 g. (⅔ oz.)	peanut powder
②	2 T.	sugar
	1 T.	lard
③	1½ T. each:	flour, water
1		bamboo mat

❶ Soak the rice until soft and steam until done (see "Bamboo Cup Rice Pudding" page 106). Mix ② with rice and divide into 3 portions.

❷ Cut the full sheet of bean curd skin into 2 halves. There should now be 3 equal sheets of bean curd skin. Cut the candied winter melon, kumquat, and fruits into equally-sized pieces. Divide the ingredients from ① into 3 equal portions.

❸ Place one bean curd skin on the bamboo mat and one portion of rice on top of that. Flatten the rice out evenly, then put one portion of ① in the middle. Roll into a long cylinder and use ③ to seal. This makes 3 rolls.

❹ Heat the oil to 100° C (200° F). Place in rolls and deep fry, over a high flame, until golden brown. Remove, drain, and cut into 3 cm. sections before serving.

6人份 Serves 6

①

②

③

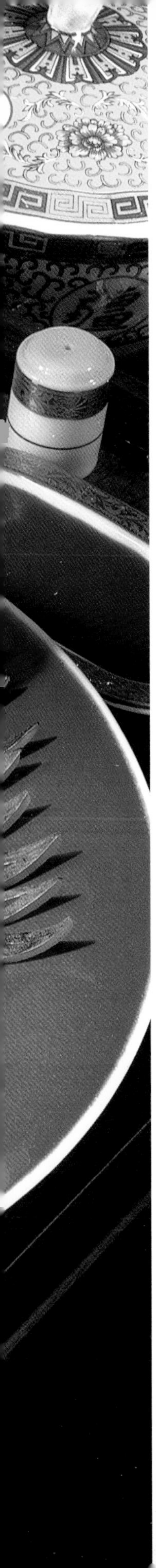

香酥雞卷

Fragrant Bean Curd Skin Roll

材料：

洋葱丁	250公克
梅花肉	100公克
洋地瓜丁、絞五花肉	各80公克
豆皮	1½張
油	5杯
太白粉	½杯
① 蕃茄醬	½大匙
鹽	¼小匙
② 魚漿	3大匙
麵粉	1大匙
麻油	½大匙
胡椒粉	1小匙
鹽、味精	各⅛小匙
五香粉、肉桂粉	各少許
③ 海山醬、鳳梨汁	各2大匙
味噌、糖	各½大匙
④ 太白粉、水	各1小匙
麵糊、糖	各1大匙

INGREDIENTS:

250 g. (8¾ oz.)		chopped onion
100 g. (3½ oz.)		pork tenderloin
80 g. (2¾ oz.) each:		chopped yam bean, ground fatty prok
1½ sheets		bean curd skin
5 c.		oil
½ c.		cornstarch
①	½ T.	ketchup
	¼ t.	salt
②	3 T.	fish paste (mashed fish)
	1 T.	flour
	½ T.	sesame oil
	1 t.	pepper
	⅛ t.	salt
	Dash each:	five spice powder, cinnamon
③	2 T. each:	"hai shan" sauce - a kind of sweet chili sauce, pineapple juice
	½ T. each:	miso, sugar
④	1 t. each:	cornstarch, water
	1 T. each:	flour-water paste, sugar

❶ 洋葱丁先以糖1大匙拌醃，擠乾水分；梅花肉洗淨，切細條狀，入①料拌勻，醃數分鐘；再拌入洋葱丁、洋地瓜丁、絞五花肉及②料為餡，分成3等份備用。

❷ 豆皮一張對切，共3小張。每張豆皮上各置1份餡（圖1），包捲成長條圓筒狀（圖2），接口處以麵糊黏緊（圖3），再沾太白粉，共做3份備用。

❸ 將油燒至5分熱（100℃，200°F），入雞卷，大火炸熟，撈起瀝油，切3公分長段排盤備用。

❹ ③料煮開，以④料勾芡，是為沾汁，食時沾之即可。

❶ Marinate the onion in 1 tablespoon of sugar and squeeze out the water. Rinse the meat clean and julienne. Marinate the meat in ① for several minutes, then mix with the onion, yam bean, ground pork and ② . This is the filling; divide it into 3 portions.

❷ Cut the whole bean curd skin in half to make a total of 3 sheets. Place 1 portion of filling on each bean curd skin (illus. 1). Roll each into a long round cylinder (illus. 2), and seal tightly with flour paste (illus. 3). Coat with the cornstarch. Make 3.

❸ Heat the oil in the wok to 100° C (200° F), then add the rolls. Deep fry over a high flame. Remove and drain. Cut into 3 cm. long sections, then arrange on a platter.

❹ Bring ③ to a boil. Stir in ④ , to thicken, and use this sauce as a dip when serving.

6人份　Serves 6

魷魚羹　Broth of Squid Soup

材料：
乾魷魚 …………………………… 1條
羹湯：
熟筍絲 ……………………… 100公克
紅蘿蔔絲、香菇絲 ……… 各40公克
柴魚 ………………………………… ½ 杯
紅葱頭 ……………………………… 4粒
油 ………………………………… 4大匙
① 鹼塊 ……………………………… 1塊
　　水 …………………………… 4杯
② 高湯 …………………………… 6杯
　　醬油、鹽 ……………… ½ 大匙
　　糖 …………………………… 1小匙
　　味精 ……………………… 少許
③ 太白粉、水 ………… 各4大匙

❶乾魷魚洗淨，續入①料浸約4小時（圖1），取出再入水中沖泡約40分鐘，去掉鹼味，取出切花片（圖2），入開水中汆燙，撈起漂凉，洗淨瀝乾備用。

❷紅葱頭切片；鍋燒熱，入油4大匙，燒至7分熱（140℃，280°F），隨入紅葱頭片，炸至金黃色，撈起瀝油，是爲油葱酥備用。

❸②料煮開，入筍絲、紅蘿蔔絲、香菇絲、柴魚，再煮開，以③料勾芡，拌入魷魚及油葱酥即可。

■食時可加沙茶醬、胡椒粉、麻油、黑醋或香菜末。

6人份　Serves 6

INGREDIENTS:
1	dried squid

Soup stock:
100 g. (3½ oz.)	julienned, canned bamboo shoots
40 g. (1⅓ oz.) each:	julienned-carrot, soaked, dried black mushrooms
½ c.	dried fish flakes
4 cloves	shallots
4 T.	oil
① { 4 t.	baking soda
4 c.	water
② { 6 c.	chicken broth
½ T. each:	soy sauce, salt
1 t.	sugar
③ 4 T. each:	cornstarch, water

❶ Rinse the squid clean. Soak in ① for about 4 hours (illus. 1), until soft. Remove, then soak in water for 40 minutes to rid squid of soda taste. Butterfly the squid (illus. 2), and slice. Scald the squid in boiling water. Remove, cool, rinse and drain.

❷ Slice the shallots. Preheat the wok, then add 4 tablespoons of oil. Heat the oil to 140° C (280° F). Add the shallots and fry until golden brown. Drain. These are fried shallot flakes.

❸ Bring ② to a boil, then add the bamboo shoots, carrots, mushrooms and fish flakes. Bring this to a boil, then stir in ③ to thicken. Stir in the squid and shallot flakes, then serve.

■ When serving, condiments such as barbeque sauce ("cha sa jiang"), pepper, sesame oil, dark vinegar or coriander may be added.

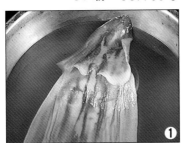

❶

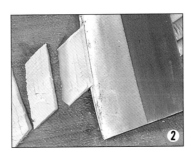

❷

香菇赤肉羹

Black Mushroom and Pork Soup

材料：

後腿肉	………………………………	240公克
魚漿	………………………………	200公克
① 酒	………………………………	1大匙
味精	………………………………	$\frac{1}{8}$小匙

羹湯：同魷魚羹（見第115頁）

❶後腿肉洗淨，切1×5公分條狀，先後拌入①料及魚漿（圖1），將肉條一一放入70℃（140℉）熱水中，再以小火燙熟（圖2），待肉條浮上來即可撈起備用。

❷羹湯煮開（作法見魷魚羹❸），拌入肉條及油葱酥即可。

INGREDIENTS:

240 g. (8½ oz.)	pork shank
200 g. (7 oz.)	fish paste (mashed fish)
① 1 T.	wine

Soup stock: Use the soup stock in "Broth of Squid Soup" (page 115).

❶ Rinse the pork clean and cut into 1×5 cm. strips. First mix with ① , then fish paste (illus. 1). Place one strip at a time in 70° C (140° F) water. Over a low flame cook the meat until done (illus. 2). When done, the meat will rise to the surface of the water. Remove from water.

❷ Follow the step ❸ directions for "Broth of Squid Soup," substituting the meat strips for squid.

6人份　Serves 6

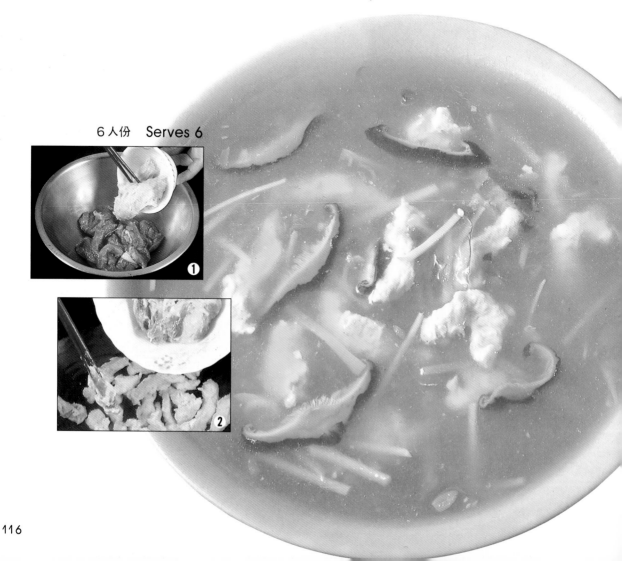

116

味全家政班

味全家政班創立於民國五十年，經過三十餘年的努力，它不只是國內歷史最悠久的家政研習班，更成為一所正式學制之外的專門學校。

創立之初，味全家政班以教授中國菜及研習烹飪技術為主，因教學成果良好，備受各界讚譽，乃於民國五十二年，增闢插花、工藝、美容等各門專科，精湛的師資，教學內容的充實，深獲海內外的肯定與好評。

三十餘年來，先後來班參與研習的學員已近二十萬人次，學員的足跡遍及台灣以外，更有許多國外的團體或個人專程抵台，到味全家政班求教，在習得中國菜烹調的精髓後，或返回居住地經營餐飲業，或擔任家政教師，或獲聘為中國餐廳主廚者大有人在，成就倍受激賞。

近年來，味全家政班亟力研究開發改良中國菜餚，並深入國際間，採集各種精緻、道地美食，除了樹立中華文化「食的精神」外，並將各國烹飪口味去蕪存菁，擷取地方特色。為了確保這些研究工作更加落實，我們特將這些集合海內外餐飲界與研發單位的精典之作，以縝密的拍攝技巧與專業編輯，出版各式食譜，以做傳承。

薪傳與發揚中國烹飪的藝術，是味全家政班一貫的理念，日後，也將秉持宗旨，永續不輟。

Wei-Chuan Cooking School

Since its establishment in 1961, Wei-Chuan Cooking School has made a continuous commitment toward improving and modernizing the culinary art of cooking and special skills training. As a result, it is the oldest and most successful school of its kind in Taiwan.

In the beginning, Wei-Chuan Cooking School was primarily teaching and researching Chinese cooking techniques. However, due to popular demand, the curriculum was expanded to cover courese in flower arrangements, handcrafts, beauty care, dress making and many other specialized fields by 1963.

The fact that almost 200,000 students, from Taiwan and other countries all over the world, have matriculated in this school can be directly attributed to the high quality of the teaching staff and the excellent curriculum provided to the studends. Many of the graduates have become successful restaurant owners and chefs, and in numerous cases, respected teachers.

While Wei-Chuan Cooking School has always been committed to developing and improving Chinese cuisine, we have recently extended our efforts toward gathering information and researching recipes from defferent provinces of China. With the same dedication to accuracy and perfection as always, we have begun to publish these authentic regional gourmet recipes for our devoted readers. These new publications will continue to reflect the fine tradition of quality our public has grown to appreciate and expect.

More Wei-Chuan Cook

純青出版社

劃撥帳號：**12106299**
地址：台北市松江路125號3樓
電話：（02）25084331・25063564
傳真：（02）25074902

Distributor: Wei-Chuan Publishing

1455 Monterey Pass Rd., #110
Monterey Park, CA 91754, U.S.A.
Tel: (213)2613880・2613878
Fax: (213)2613299

健康食譜
- 100道菜
- 120頁
- 中英對照

Healthful Cooking
- 100 recipes
- 120 pages
- Chinese/English Bilingual

素食
- 84道菜
- 120頁
- 中英對照

Vegetarian Cooking
- 84 recipes
- 120 pages
- Chinese/English Bilingual

健康素
- 76道菜
- 96頁
- 中英對照

Simply Vegetarian
- 76 recipes
- 96 pages
- Chinese/English Bilingual

微波食譜第一冊
- 62道菜
- 112頁
- 中英對照

Microwave Cooking Chinese Style
- 62 recipes
- 112 pages
- Chinese/English Bilingual

微波食譜第二冊
- 76道菜
- 128頁
- 中英對照

Microwave Cooking Chinese Style 2
- 76 recipes
- 128 pages
- Chinese/English Bilingual

美味小菜
- 92道菜
- 96頁
- 中英對照

Appetizers
- 92 recipes
- 96 pages
- Chinese/English Bilingual

實用烘焙
- 77道點心
- 96頁
- 中英對照

International Baking Delight
- 77 recipes
- 96 pages
- Chinese/English Bilingual

飲茶食譜
- 88道菜
- 128頁
- 中英對照

Chinese Dim Sum
- 88 recipes
- 128 pages
- Chinese/English Bilingual

養生藥膳
- 73道菜
- 128頁
- 中英對照

Chinese Herb Cooking for Health
- 73 recipes
- 128 pages
- Chinese/English Bilingual

廣東菜
- 75道菜
- 96頁
- 中英對照

Chinese Cuisine Cantonese Style
- 75 recipes
- 96 pages
- Chinese/English Bilingual

Books

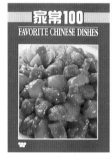

家常菜
- ● 226道菜
- ● 200頁
- ● 中文版

營養便當
- ● 147道菜
- ● 96頁
- ● 中文版

嬰幼兒食譜
- ● 140道菜
- ● 104頁
- ● 中文版

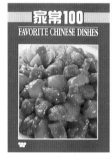

米食-家常篇
- ● 84道菜
- ● 96頁
- ● 中英對照

米食-傳統篇
- ● 82道菜
- ● 96頁
- ● 中英對照

麵食-家常篇
- ● 91道菜
- ● 96頁
- ● 中英對照

麵食-精華篇
- ● 87道菜
- ● 96頁
- ● 中英對照

家常100
- ● 100道菜
- ● 96頁
- ● 中英對照

Rice
Home Cooking
- ● 84 recipes
- ● 96 pages
- ● Chinese/English Bilingual

Rice
Traditional Cooking
- ● 82 recipes
- ● 96 pages
- ● Chinese/English Bilingual

Noodles
Home Cooking
- ● 91 recipes
- ● 96 pages
- ● Chinese/English Bilingual

Noodles
Classical Cooking
- ● 87 recipes
- ● 96 pages
- ● Chinese/English Bilingual

Favorite Chinese Dishes
- ● 100 recipes
- ● 96 pages
- ● Chinese/English Bilingual

四川菜
- ● 115道菜
- ● 96頁
- ● 中英對照

上海菜
- ● 91道菜
- ● 96頁
- ● 中英對照

台灣菜
- ● 73道菜
- ● 120頁
- ● 中英對照

庖廚偏方 庖廚錦囊 庖廚樂
- ●中文版

Chinese Cuisine
Szechwan Style
- ● 115 recipes
- ● 96 pages
- ● Chinese/English Bilingual

Chinese Cuisine
Shanghai Style
- ● 91 recipes
- ● 96 pages
- ● Chinese/English Bilingual

Chinese Cuisine
Taiwanese Style
- ● 73 recipes
- ● 120 pages
- ● Chinese/English Bilingual

低塩、甘脆
吃不膩！
LESS SALT、CRUNCHY
WITH A TASTE
THAT NEVER TIRES.

味全上口罐頭系列
wei-chuan shang-ko can foods series.